About this book

Why is this topic important?

In some ways, instructional design missed the boat. Powerful authoring tools coupled with the Internet and low-cost, media-capable computers expanded the sea of instructional possibilities dramatically and did so almost in an instant. Both synchronous and asynchronous communication capabilities exploded and also brought interactive, multimedia-capable mobile devices into the mix. Experienced instructional designers find guidance lacking in classical literature and design principles, while inexperienced designers are drowning in alluring capabilities.

What can you achieve with this book?

You are looking at a lifesaver. This book redirects and narrows the focus of instructional design to those things that matter most in creating successful e-learning applications. Interactive media possibilities easily swamp well-intentioned efforts and reinforce the tendency of organizations to focus on the presentation of information. But with this book, you'll find not only effective ways to design meaningful, memorable, and motivational experiences. You'll also find a blending of successful behavioral change principles. Based on dozens of research studies, these principles will help you design learning events that go far beyond the transmission of information to achieve behavioral change and targeted performance levels.

How is this book organized?

This book is divided into three parts.

Part I   Scenarios

> These short scenarios capture common situations in which instructional designers often find themselves. The decisions designers made are listed for you to judge before you read Parts II and III, so you can assess your approach and instincts against thoughts presented in this book.

Part II The Art and Science of Instructional Design—
A Balanced View

    Research, theories, and popular approaches are identified and
discussed as a backdrop for presenting the Success-Based Design
techniques discussed in the remainder of the book. The need to
prepare learners for learning and to assist them in transferring new
abilities to applied performance mandates a design perspective
that's expands outside the box of simply preparing learning
modules.

Part III Designing Successful e-Learning

    The chapters of Part III step through each phase of learning and
stage of behavioral change, presenting applicable instructional
design concepts and techniques. A matrix of the components of
interactivity (context, challenge, activity, and feedback) crossed
over the critical characteristics of learning events (meaningful,
memorable, and motivational) provides the structure.

About the library series

After success with Authorware, Inc. and Macromedia, I felt that I had made a contribution to learning that would satisfy me through retirement. And retire Mary Ann and I did . . . for a few months.

But as my colleagues and I observed what happened with tools that made development of interactive learning systems so much easier to master, it was clear the job wasn't done. Instead of wondrously varied instructional paradigms burgeoning forth, offering more learning fun and effectiveness to the benefit of people and organizations everywhere, we found dry, boring, pedantic presentation of content followed by posttests. The very model of instruction that was drudgery without technology was being replicated and inflicted on ever greater numbers of captive audiences.

Making technology easier to use provided the means, but not the guidance, necessary to use it well. To atone for this gross oversight on my part, I formed Allen Interactions in 1993 with a few of my closest and most talented friends in e-learning. Our mission was and is to help everyone and anyone produce better technology-enhanced learning experiences. We established multiple studios within our company so that these teams of artisans could build long-term relationships with each other and their clients. Studios develop great internal efficiencies and, most importantly, get to understand their clients' organizations and performance needs intimately—sometimes better than clients understand them themselves.

Although our studios compete in the custom development arena, we also share our best practices openly and freely. We exhibit our applications as openly as clients allow, hoping they will stimulate critique and discussion so we can all do better and so successful ideas can be broadly applied. We teach and mentor in-house organizations that aspire to create great learning applications. And, in close association with the American Society for Training & Development (ASTD), we offer certificate programs to help participants develop effective design and development skills.

This series of books is another way we are doing our best to help advance the field of technology-enhanced learning. I've not intentionally held back any secrets in putting forth the best practices our studios are continually enhancing.

This, the second book in the series, presents an expanded view of instruction, looking not only at the key factors of successful learning experiences, but also at what influences learners and performers before, during, and after instruction. Six books are planned for this library, each to be focused on one major aspect of the process of designing and developing great e-learning applications. I plan to address learner interface design, project management, deployment, and more. When the series is compiled, I hope it will be a useful tool for developing great and valuable learning experiences.

Michael Allen's e-Learning Library

Pfeiffer™

Michael Allen's e-Learning Library

Designing Successful e-Learning

Forget What You Know About Instructional Design and Do Something Interesting

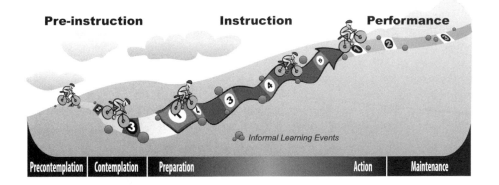

Michael W. Allen

BICENTENNIAL
1807
WILEY
2007
BICENTENNIAL

John Wiley & Sons, Inc.

Published by Pfeiffer
An Imprint of Wiley
989 Market Street, San Francisco, CA 94103-1741
www.pfeiffer.com

For additional copies/bulk purchases of this book in the U.S. please contact 800-274-4434.

Pfeiffer books and products are available through most bookstores. To contact Pfeiffer directly call our Customer Care Department within the U.S. at 800-274-4434, outside the U.S. at 317-572-3985, fax 317-572-4002, or visit www.pfeiffer.com.

Pfeiffer also publishes its books in a variety of electronic formats. Some content that appears in print may not be available in electronic books.

ISBN 978-0-7879-8299-7

Cover photo of Michael Allen by Courtney Platt, Grand Cayman, B.W.I.

Contents

Acknowledgments

Successful instructional design is a challenging and complex undertaking. Making headway toward a clear understanding of the process and successful principles requires the collaboration of many experienced and insightful minds. To all those people who have schooled me and shared their wisdom, I give my thanks. To the many organizations that have given my colleagues and me the opportunity to work on their behalf toward improved learning and performance, I also give my thanks.

We are all indebted to James Prochaska, John Norcross, and Carlo DiClemente for their work on behavioral change, which provides helpful explanations for and insights into the disappointing results of many learning interventions.

In the preparation of this work, I am particularly indebted to Richard Sites, Carla Torgerson, and Julie Dirksen for their help and insights. Ethan Edwards, Edmond Manning, Doug Bratland, Len Eichten, Chad Worcester, Stephen Rekstad, Jason Zeaman, Will Thalheimer, and Susan Taylor all made invaluable contributions. Michael Gause coordinated schedules, tasks, documents, updates, and communications. Christopher Allen designed and laid out the book. Corey Stern provided illustrations. Marty Lipshutz and John Welsh provided excellent counsel while taking on extra responsibilities so I could focus on the project.

Special thanks to Nancy Olson at ASTD for her unfailing enthusiasm for developing this material and coordinating the certificate programs based on it.

As always, there is no way to thank my family enough for their patience and support during the extended periods of time during which I was either physically or just mentally off working on the manuscript. Preparation of these books is always a more demanding undertaking than I anticipate. Mary Ann's encouragement and confidence in me joins an unwavering patience that few spouses are privileged to have. We both hope sincerely that this publication shares meaningful, memorable, and motivational thoughts.

For Steve Birth whose programming talent made "impossible" features in Authorware a reality and whose life is even more exemplary than his programming.

For Carl Philabaum whose interface design talent remains unequalled and whose perspectives on computing brings me hope.

Foreword

I was very pleased when Michael Allen asked me to write a foreword for his new book, *Designing Successful e-Learning*. Michael Allen is an e-learning pioneer who has a deep knowledge and tremendous experience in designing world-class e-learning solutions. Because of his passion to move the advancement of e-learning to the next level, he shares with the reader his unique expertise, specific insights, and concrete examples for designing effective online learning.

In this foreword, first we'll discuss a conceptual framework that provides a continuum of online learning capabilities, then preview the contribution Michael Allen's new book offers to our collective abilities to produce learning that is *meaningful, memorable, and motivational,* and finally explore a snapshot of the future of learning in a virtual world.

When I published the English edition of *The e-Learning Fieldbook* in 2004 (www.elearningfieldbook. com), e-learning was in the initial developmental stages. I gathered case examples of leading practices in major Fortune companies and organizations worldwide and found that one of the most critical success factors for the adoption of e-learning is **the capability to design high quality and effective e-learning.** In reviewing a large number of e-learning programs launched over the years, I am still convinced that this is one of the key and most interesting challenges for all e-learning professionals.

Four years ago, there were many projections that the e-learning field would experience exponential growth. These forecasts have actually been surpassed due to a great extent by the seminal work of pioneers like Michael Allen in maximizing the quality and effectiveness of e-learning design.

Online Learning Continuum

*It is a real page-turner…*usually describes an exciting, dynamic *who-done-it* novel that keeps you engaged from the first moment right up to the last page. However, the early world of e-learning produced exactly the opposite, e-learning courses with limited instructional design— *e-reading page-turners* or PowerPoint® slides that were read online, with limited interaction and no dynamic exchanges. Learners engaged in this type of e-learning were disillusioned and initially turned off about learning online.

This experience supported my firm belief that e-learning excellence requires the right investment in instructional design, founded on proven didactical/learning theories and principles. The Online Learning Continuum figure below depicts applications of e-learning methods that support effective learning and the design requirements at each stage.

As you move along the continuum from e-reading to e-learning, it is important to note that the degree of investment in instructional design increases the further out you move. Simulations, gaming, and scenario-based e-learning courses are the most powerful learning experiences, because they provide people with opportunities to do the

job in a simulated environment. Designing this level of e-learning solutions requires a combination of well-educated and experienced e-learning designers who have a drive to enhance the e-learning experience, the right design and development methods and tools, and last but not least, sufficient design and development time. This can result in high-impact e-learning solutions that are dynamic, engaging, fun, and effective.

Why is the book important?

As a leader in applying the theories of behavioural, cognitive, humanistic, and social theory to the development and design of e-learning programs, Michael believes that online learning must surpass a course focus to include all of the stages of growth and development required to generate behavioral change—the ultimate outcome of learning. His focus embraces the complete online learning process from pre-program online learning investments, through excellent e-learning course design, to post-program actions that embed the learning in new behaviors.

The theoretical literature on learning and growth can be difficult to master and even more challeng-

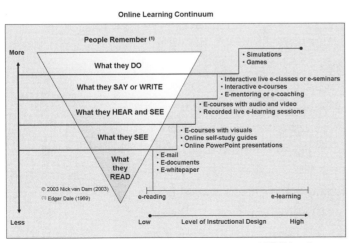

Online Learning Continuum

© 2003 Nick van Dam

ing to integrate into e-learning, but Michael has made this easy for all of us. He explains this thinking in clear and accessible language, amplifies the theories with research results, and describes popular approaches by applying these theories to learning and growth. Taking the illustrations even further into the field of e-learning design, he offers useful scenarios and practical examples of how these theories can be employed in online learning programs, providing readers with concrete ideas to leverage them in their own work.

Where does e-learning go from here?

A myriad of online learning solutions have emerged over recent years, including self-paced e-learning, virtual classrooms, simulations, games, and communities of practices,

A number of integrated learning solutions provide people with access to information/knowledge over time and support the e-learning design advocated by Michael Allen. Whereas people in the past searched in books and with colleagues and friends for knowledge, today Google has become the *killer application* for learning. Podcasting, both for sound and video, has been launched

Spectrum of Formal and Workplace Learning

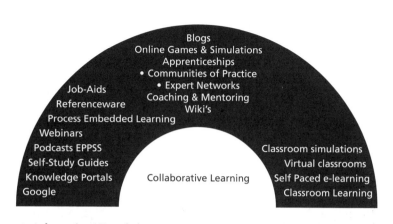

by many enterprises and proven to be a very effective medium too for sharing knowledge with a younger generation, as universities are leveraging the ubiquitous iPod® and its competitors to provide students with access to curricula and online lectures.

Collaborative learning applications, including communities of practice, expert networks, and online simulations, are experiencing rapid growth and will have a strong future as they support the team-based learning style of Generation Internet. The classroom has been transformed in many organizations from lecture-based and PowerPoint-driven events toward a facilitated learning continuum. Classroom simulations and expert performance coaching provide people with a real work experience in a safe environment and support the integration of new behaviors into the workplace.

Most enterprises are in the process of defining a new learning strategy that will provide knowledge and skills to their people when they need it. All learning solutions shown in the visual above will be part of this extended blend of learning.

Personally, I am convinced that the next generation of e-learning solutions will be 3-D virtual learning environments comparable to Second Life (www.secondlife.com). Second Life is a 3-D global virtual world built and owned entirely by its residents. Since opening to the public in 2003, it has grown explosively and is inhabited by millions of people from around the globe. Even the U.S. presidential race has town meetings inhabited by avatars of the candidates and joined-in by residents of the virtual world. In the

business world, these 3-D learning environments will include employee avatars and will provide the learner with a complete, real, interactive, and collaborative learning experience that is completely learner-centric.

Very interesting times ahead of us all—but it's clear to me that emerging technologies will provide new opportunities for developing e-learning solutions. However, they will only be adopted and successfully implemented if solid instructional design methods and human cognitive and behavioral learning practices have been applied.

I hope that you will enjoy this book and will apply the knowledge in your daily work, taking e-learning to the next level.

Nick van Dam, Ph.D.
Global Chief Learning Officer for Deloitte
Founder & Chairman,
e-Learning For Kids Foundation
www.e-learningforkids.org

Preface

Writing a short book on instructional design is difficult. Just as Mark Twain mused that he didn't have time to write a short letter and so wrote a long one, this short book took me far longer to write then I anticipated. But it also took me to points of interest I didn't anticipate with results I find exciting.

I didn't want to simply restate points I've made in previous books, no matter how important and valid I think they are and no matter how often people ignore them, gleefully creating boring and dreadful learning experiences aplenty. Those points are made as well as I know how, and while I do revisit some of them in this book, I wanted this series to move forward, as I hope my own thinking about e-learning and instructional design is.

The perspective of forgetting what you "know" about instructional design is helpful because in creating e-learning that doesn't work and is, indeed, so often boring, designers frequently defend their decisions based on what they feel is solid knowledge about how design should be done or about how humans learn. I don't often find myself disagreeing about the referenced research, but if the science is true and the e-learning are poor, there's a problem in translating principles to application.

Problems often occur in generalization. *A study reports that learners preferred narration of on-screen text; therefore, narration should always accompany on-screen text.* Of course, that's not always true or a good design decision. One has to be extremely careful and thoughtful in translating research findings to practice. The proof is, of course, "in the pudding." If the e-learning is ineffective, the design wasn't good, no matter how defensible referenced research may be.

In this book, I've tried to combine the two poles of wisdom—what we know from research and what we know from experience—to create a core set of recommendations and guidelines. In developing this approach, I discovered something I think is truly profound, exciting, and practical. It's the Stages of Change model by James Prochaska, John Norcoss, and Carlo DiClemente developed from a meta study of research done on how humans change their behavior patterns. This research strongly suggests that for people to change their behavior they must traverse well-defined stages in a specific sequence.

If they do not satisfy the requirements of each stage, any observable changes will be short-lived. The model lists techniques that have proven successful in helping people work through the stages and achieve behavioral change.

As we look at this model from the instructional point of view, it points out the need to prepare learners for change before we begin teaching them how to change. And it points out how we must assist learners after they have begun to apply new skills so that they won't fall back into less desirable behavior patterns. This perspective demands that we design outside the box of instructional modules and think more broadly about the things influencing learners before (Pre-instruction phase), during (Instruction phase), and after instruction (Performance phase). By taking a broader perspective, we can see how blending e-learning technologies with informal learning, learning support, and performance support can strongly increase the prospects of achieving performance success.

Finally, I took another look at two powerful concepts I've introduced in previous books and presentations:

1) interactive events are constructed of four components—context, challenge, activity, and feedback, and 2) instructional events must be meaningful, memorable, and motivational to achieve desired results. In this book, I've combined these concepts into a 4 x 3 matrix to provide a structure for discussing specific design guidelines that seem, in my practice, to be successful time and time again.

There has long been a problem of how to discuss instructional design. We are crippled by the lack of a generally understood vocabulary about instructional design, and therefore, when people discuss designs, they often feel they're in agreement when it later turns out they were far from it. I think the matrix helps by providing a conceptual language designers can use to talk both among themselves and with other stakeholders about design decisions.

I hope you'll find the perspectives and tools introduced in this book helpful as you move your own thinking about instructional design forward.

February 6, 2007
MWA

Part One
Real-World Contexts

Believing that learning experiences are most interesting when they begin with a challenge—not a daunting challenge, not a potentially embarrassing experience, but a challenge that immediately focuses learners on the task at hand and shows them they have applicable skills (if they do) and that there's still something to learn (if there is)—we begin Part One with a set of very modest challenges.

The first three challenges are embedded in scenarios drawn from experience with organizations that are searching for ways to be effective with e-learning. For each scenario, I've listed design principles these organizations have put forth to guide their work. Some of the principles obviously came from traditional instructional design curricula. Others came from personal preference, an intuitive sense of what would be best, or who knows where. Sometimes, I'm truly mystified.

I'm asking for your opinion of each principle proposed before you read what I have to say about it. Some of the listed principles I can support; others I find problematic. I'm sure you will too. You and I might agree, I might change your mind, and I might not. In work that's as creative as e-learning, where we are working with many variables, there are few indisputable rights and wrongs. Even what might seem to be a ridiculous shortcut, such as "give no feedback," can be an excellent principle in some circumstances. While there is a great body of research to draw from, the innumerable variety of circumstances designers contend with makes instructional design much more of a problem-solving practice than a technology.

The question is: What would you do?

In This Part

What I hope to do in this part is get you thinking and questioning. Few people believe e-learning is achieving its potential. Too much of it is embarrassingly bad from almost any point of view. But there are times when it has provided amazing learning experiences—experiences that have changed individual lives, opened the door to new careers, and helped organizations not only survive, but achieve spectacular bottom-line performance. This potential would be too great an opportunity to ignore, even if e-learning weren't so attractive because of its ability to reduce instructional costs.

This book is all about questioning what we think we know about instructional design. It's far more important that designs lead to successful performance than comply with tradition, principle, or theory. So think about the principles listed in the first three scenarios and note what you think about them.

In Scenario 4, I'm asking you to list your most cherished design principles. I'm only looking for ten. If you're an experienced designer, you'll have trouble reducing your list to just ten, although as you begin to list them with a questioning mind, you might feel like withdrawing a few that seemed like good candidates at first. If you're new to the field, you might have trouble coming up with ten, but just think about the learning experiences you thought were exceptionally good and draw principles from them. You can also draw from the ideas in the previous scenarios. Try to come up with ten if you possibly can.

Scenario 1: Hoboken Automotive Devices

Hoboken Automotive Devices excitedly launched new interactive courses on leadership, performance evaluation, and sexual harassment in 2005. Their internal team of ten people, plus almost as many external independent contractors, designed and built the courses following the successive approximation protocol. They had never tried this method before, but resolving a few points of confusion here and there only brought deeper appreciation for the process.

Margaret Applegate was named project manager. She received her master's degree in instructional design six years ago, earning almost straight As. She's been working as a technical writer and instructional designer at Hoboken for almost ten years and has rolled out numerous electronic reference manuals and interactive user guides.

To make sure they didn't waste their funds, course designs were consistent, and quality standards were met, Margaret set criteria for their e-learning projects. Among Margaret's requirements were the following:

➤ Courses will be broken down into short modules, rarely requiring a learner to spend more than twenty minutes to complete each one.

➤ Behavioral outcome objectives will be listed for learners at the beginning of each module.

➤ Lessons will be highly interactive, requiring frequent user input. Game formats, such as Jeopardy or Wheel of Fortune, should be used to keep learner interest high.

➤ To gain positive learner reactions, learner errors should be minimized.

➤ Task concepts and processes are presented clearly and demonstrated before learners are asked to perform them.

➤ To make the procedures covered in the courses workable as corporate standards, content must be complete and suitable for new employees as well as for recurrent training.

The review committee was very excited about the courses from both a content and design point of view. The interactive games were clever, the overall graphic appearance was fresh and energetic, and the content seemed to be exactly right. Initial reviews from employees were very positive.

What's your take?

Do you think Hoboken Automotive Devices is successful with their e-learning under Margaret's direction?

O Yes

O No

If No, why not?

For each of Margaret's requirements below, check whether you think it was a good idea or a bad one. Note why you think his requirements are good or bad or what you would do:

1. Courses are broken down into short modules, rarely requiring a learner to spend more than twenty minutes to complete each one.

O Good

O Bad

O Don't Know

Why?

2. Behavioral outcome objectives are listed for learners at the beginning of each module.

O Good

O Bad

O Don't Know

Why?

3. Lessons are highly interactive, requiring frequent user input. Game formats, such as Jeopardy or Wheel of Fortune, are used to keep learner interest high.

○ Good

○ Bad

○ Don't Know

Why?

4. To gain positive learner reactions, challenge difficulty is kept low to minimize incorrect answers.

○ Good

○ Bad

○ Don't Know

Why?

5. Task concepts and processes are presented clearly and demonstrated before learners are asked to perform them.

○ Good

○ Bad

○ Don't Know

Why?

6. To make the procedures covered in the courses workable as corporate standards, content must be complete and suitable for new employees as well as for recurrent training.

○ Good

○ Bad

○ Don't Know

Why?

Scenario 2: Water Mountain Beverage Company

Ichiro of Water Mountain Beverage Company has always been a meticulous instructional designer—organized, punctual, and charismatic. Everyone trusts Ichiro, both those inside and outside the training department. Trainers have confidence in Ichiro's experience and his ready knowledge of learning research. Division leaders actually recognize their naiveté about instruction, but feel that because Ichiro is in charge, their training is superior to the competition's and gives them a competitive advantage.

e-Learning at Water Mountain Beverage Company is used widely. It has saved significant training expenses. It has saved so much, in fact, that they now develop and deliver about three times the amount of training offered in the past, and training expenses still total less than before. Employees accept e-learning, although they often have to be coerced to take it. There are plenty of jokes about things they find poorly done, and everybody shares cheat sheets to minimize the time needed to complete lessons.

Ichiro has used successive approximation—the process detailed in the first book of this library—for some projects, especially where there are political sensitivities in the organization and where courses have high visibility. But he doesn't like the level of control he gives up in the process. After all, personnel supervisors aren't instructional designers. Why should their opinions about content and interactivity be debated? It just wastes time.

Ichiro prefers the manageability of gathering information, completing a needs analysis, performing a task assessment, choosing appropriate media, storyboarding the design, getting the thing built, and rolling out the instruction. It's hard and complicated, but he knows how to get it done. He likes the expediency of letting each specialist do what he or she does best, and getting on with it.

But successive approximation has yielded some project wins for him. When he knows a project is ill conceived, for whatever reason, he uses successive approximation. The multilevel support successive approximation builds at the beginning of the process usually overcomes any problems he anticipates. He somewhat resents the success of these projects, however, because their success often stems from the enthusiasm that builds up during the design and development process—not because of his superior design work. People outside the training department jump in with great incentives for learners and high levels of post-training support. They talk up the training program, generating enthusiasm for it even before programs are available. How fair was that?

In one successive approximation project, the team decided that providing some high-level simulations were worth the costs, and they upped the original budget. Again, Ichiro thought that wasn't a fair comparison to his streamlined approach, in which he always works within the budget provided. Besides, he would recommend development of more costly components himself if he thought his boss would listen, understand, and approve the budget.

Ichiro doesn't argue that successive approximation takes longer. He's learned otherwise, although it seemed like it would take longer when he first gave it a try. No, his primary objection is letting so many people outside his department get involved and then having to respectfully explain why their ideas about training aren't good. Either way, he always manages to come up with good designs and get valuable organizational support, but it's tiresome trying to explain principles of good instruction over and over again. He prefers focusing that time and energy on designing applications.

Ichiro now has a standard method of handling all projects. At initial team meetings, Ichiro outlines "good" design principles he expects to be followed. They include:

> ➤ Clearly and accurately identify what learners need to know.
> ➤ Prepare posttests concurrent with (or even preceding) development of presentation content, so everyone will know what the target is.

- ➤ Use a modular structure with each module consisting of the following items in sequence: introduction, outline of basic points, elaboration of basic points, exercises with mentoring and available reference material, and posttest.
- ➤ Make text pages complete, accurate, and readable.
- ➤ Graduate exercises from easy to hard and precede each new type of problem or exercise with a demonstration.
- ➤ Provide immediate corrective feedback for each error and immediate confirmation of each correct response.

What's your take?

Do you think Water Mountain Beverage Company is successful with their e-learning using Ichiro's design principles?

○ Yes

○ No

If No, why not?

For each of Ichiro's requirements below, check whether you think it was a good idea or a bad one. Note why you think his requirements are good or bad or what you would do:

1. Clearly and accurately identify what learners need to know.

○ Good

○ Bad

○ Don't Know

Why?

2. Prepare posttests concurrent with (or even preceding) development of presentation content, so everyone will know what the target is.

○ Good

○ Bad

○ Don't Know

Why?

3. Use a modular structure with each module consisting of the following items in sequence: introduction, outline of basic points, elaboration of basic points, exercises with mentoring and available reference material, and posttest.

○ Good

○ Bad

○ Don't Know

Why?

4. Make text pages complete, accurate, and readable.

○ Good

○ Bad

○ Don't Know

Why?

5. Graduate exercises from easy to hard and precede each new type of problem or exercise with a demonstration.

○ Good

○ Bad

○ Don't Know

Why?

6. Provide immediate corrective feedback for each error and immediate confirmation of each correct response.

○ Good

○ Bad

○ Don't Know

Why?

Scenario 3: Top Tech Temps

Bill Hamm's introduction as the new head of the e-Learning Group came as a big surprise to the employees in the group. Coming from outside the company, he wasn't familiar with the way things were done at Top Tech Temps. And he wasn't hesitant about his intent to make changes.

"I'm delighted to be part of this organization. I'm impressed with the talents you have individually and collectively, and I have complete confidence that we can begin designing and developing superior e-learning for TTT almost immediately," he said.

"As you may or may not know, management has been trying to decide whether to continue with e-learning or to revert back completely to instructor-led learning. Although the reduced costs of not needing classroom facilities, travel, and instructors have been beneficial, the costs of e-learning seem to be going up and up. Even so, trainees continue to lack performance skills needed to serve clients without extensive hand-holding after they've completed their e-learning.

"This has been discussed with the leadership of this group on several occasions, but the response has always been something about needing to hire better employees. I'm sure most of you have a different opinion. We've got a year to demonstrate a big change, or we're all out. Here's what we're going to do:

> ➤ Each project will have a marketing director who is responsible for creating corporate awareness and enthusiasm for the training program and what it will create.

> ➤ Each project will have a Mentoring and Performance Evaluation Program (MPEP) director.

> ➤ From a product point of view, we will develop for each project the following three components:
> 1. A pre-instruction program to help learners prepare for learning and commit to excellent post-training support, even before they've begun training.

2. A training program that's as simple and interactive as possible. Every module of instruction will be meaningful, memorable, and motivational.

3. Training to prepare supervisors for their role in a Mentoring and Performance Evaluation Program (MPEP).

Bill pointed out that there were costs for the expanded components he was requiring, so the group would be expected to produce no more than half as many projects as they had in the past couple of years.

"Next year, however, I have no doubt that we'll move up on the learning curve and be able to produce significantly more projects. And, most importantly, we'll have a very high level of enthusiastic support for what we're doing at all levels of the company."

What's your take?

Do you think Bill's initiatives brought e-learning success to Top Tech Temps?	O Yes O No	If No, why not?

For each of Bill's requirements below, check whether you think it was a good idea or a bad one. Note why you think his requirements are good or bad or what you would do:

1. Each project will have a marketing director who is responsible for creating corporate awareness and enthusiasm for the training program and what it will create.	O Good O Bad O Don't Know	Why?

2. Each project will have a Mentoring and Performance Evaluation Program (MPEP) director.

○ Good

○ Bad

○ Don't Know

Why?

3. Each project will include a pre-instruction program to help learners prepare for learning and commit to excellent post-training support, even before they've begun training.

○ Good

○ Bad

○ Don't Know

Why?

4. Each project will include a training program that's as simple and interactive as possible. Every module of instruction will be meaningful, memorable,

○ Good

○ Bad

○ Don't Know

Why?

Scenario 4: Bellmore University

You have just joined Bellmore University. Yes, you. (Ok, play along with me here.) You've joined as an assistant professor in the Department of Instructional Technologies, where you will be creating a new curriculum on instructional design.

You would like the curriculum to exemplify many of the tenets you espouse about instructional design and the use of technology to assist learning. You have to be realistic, of course. You don't have a lot of money to spend in development and will actually be working with graduate student assistants to develop the e-learning applications as well as any other materials needed. With the funding you have, you will be able to spend a year working on design and development before the first course must be offered.

Having assembled a team of five teaching assistants, three of whom have advanced interactive multimedia development skills, you begin by describing the design attributes you think are most important. You know many details will have to be discussed later and you can't outline everything that's important in this first meeting, so you present the following list as the most important characteristics and elements as you see them initially.

It's a challenge, I know, but write (on the following pages) your ten top requirements (if you can think of ten) before reading the next two parts of this book. Feel free to reference the requirements listed in Scenarios 1-3 and include any of them you feel belong in your own top ten.

Part I

Your Requirements	Reason for Requirement
1.	
2.	
3.	
4.	
5.	

6.

7.

8.

9.

10.

Part Two

The Art & Science of Instructional Design

We want our house to stand the test of time, I told the architect. After Macromedia went public, we had a chance to build our dream home. This was going to be the house we always wanted. Perhaps it would be in our family for generations. But defining and merging dreams is a lot more difficult than having a pleasant sleep.

We had the solution. The exterior would be a style that has kept its appeal for centuries. We were fairly flexible on this and easily settled on French Country, with brick, stone, and tall French doors.

The interior, now that's where we could be trendy. We went for soft contemporary—a compromise between the contemporary designs I like and the softer, homey look my wife loves. We both like antiques and how they blend with modern art, so we had a happy solution.

We engaged a talented architect who loved challenge. He came up with lots of creative and very much unexpected ideas for the interior. "The foyer should have exposed brick walls. A rough metal shelf or ledge with angular brackets will hide the up lighting. The main hallway floor will be made of old glass bricks and have iron grates in it. Rooms will be placed at odd angles to each other. The walls will have industrial horizontal grooves."

With each suggestion, I was the one who objected. "I don't want to live in a factory," I pled. He quietly acquiesced through every rejection without protest.

One day, as we were agonizing about some finish detail, I saw a blueprint and sketches upside down on his desk. It was amazing. When I asked him who was the lucky owner, he said, "This was your house as I had envisioned it."

How do professional instructional designers overcome the pressures of stakeholders, the challenges of design, and unsuccessful traditions?

Many people who have e-learning design responsibilities today have had little to no formal instructional design training. They take guidance from what others are doing and from their experiences as learners. I've been to the dentist many times, but you wouldn't want me attempting to fill a tooth cavity in your mouth, I assure you. Just being around professionals doesn't make you one. Being a student doesn't make you a teacher.

At the same time, many well-educated instructional designers who have not worked with interactive technologies attempt to apply designs that don't translate well from the classroom or textbook to e-learning. The medium really does demand different design decisions, and there are important skills to be mastered if one is to become a successful e-learning designer.

In this part, we look briefly at instructional design as it is practiced today with, admittedly, a somewhat critical eye. Because the potential of e-learning is so great and the realization of this potential so infrequent (although noticeably improving), we have to wonder whether the most popular approaches are well founded.

We then move on to basic principles of successful design and finally add a new perspective that shows great promise—that of understanding how we can help learners prepare themselves for learning, commit to improved performance, and apply newly learned skills successfully.

Chapter 5—What is Instructional Design?

We overview instructional design together with its purpose and traditions, both before e-learning and in today's context. We identify some of the leading theories and approaches as a basis for introducing the design approaches recommended throughout the remainder of the book.

Major topics include:

The design challenge
The big questions
New challenges
Systematic process
Art or science?
Education versus training
Knowing versus doing
Alternative design approaches
    Intuitive
    Research and Theory-based
    Behaviorism
    Cognitivism
    Constructivism

Chapter 6—Success-Based Design

Success-based design is an eclectic approach sporting principles that have been observed in successful application across a wide range of projects. The principles are drawn from many different sources. Some were discovered simply by luck, but most were taken from theory, research, or experience.

Major topics include:

Making good decisions

The three Ms

   M1: Meaningful learning experiences

   M2: Memorable learning experiences

   M3: Motivational learning experiences

The fourth M: Measurable results

Characteristics of successful designs

A practical and realistic guide

Chapter 7—Designing Outside the Box

If the purpose of e-learning is to enable success, and if success comes from doing the right things at the right times, then e-learning needs to focus on the real-world factors that determine behavior. Those factors include much more than the things people know. They include experiences that may have occurred long before encountering our instructional programs and influences that exist afterward in the performance environment.

The psychology of behavioral change has much to offer instructional designers. Analysis of many research investigations suggests that there is an inviolable sequence of stages people move through in order to change their behaviors, especially when bad habits are in conflict with desired behavior. In this chapter, we align the stages of change with the three major phases of learning to provide a primary structure for discussing instructional design.

Major topics include:

Buried in a box

Broader perspectives

Working the larger contexts

   Pre-instruction phase

   Instruction phase

   Performance phase

   Accumulating influences

The design challenge

The psychology of behavioral change

Stages of Change model

Parallels to learning for performance improvement

Aligning stages of change

Implications for instructional design
Expanding the purview of instruc-
tional design
Spaced learning events
Informal learning
Blended learning

5 | What Is Instructional Design?

My Uncle Tommy was smart. Witty too. After working with my dad at his printing company for several years, he set off to the northeast to explore metropolitan life. He landed a career-long position with Eastman Kodak with responsibility for the information sheets and manuals that came with their film and camera products.

Uncle Tommy gave me a photographer's used camera when I was only about twelve years old. Ironically, he didn't have the manual for it but promised he'd deliver instructional materials the following day. I didn't wait (as was apparently expected) and shot up all eight rolls of film he had given me. I completely ruined seven by not having set proper exposures, but the eighth roll turned out reasonably well.

My dad was upset with me, but my uncle seemed fascinated. Because of the tension—

my dad ready to inflict punishment, and my uncle acting like I was about to win a medal—I'll never forget what Uncle T said:

"You've done what most of our customers do, ignore the instructions and start pushing buttons and turning dials. Of course, you didn't really have a choice, but you were learning without much feedback at all. And you were doing it before the instructions could dissipate your enthusiasm. Now if we could only find a way to keep the fun and excitement high while we help our customers learn the fundamental concepts of cameras and photography."

The world is instructive

Instructive, but dangerous. Fire is hot. Unrestrained objects fall to the ground. Sarcastic comments expedite little goodwill. We learn all these things and much more without the hand of the instructional designer. Singeing the skin, shattering a priceless vase, and being fired for poor attitude may be dramatically instructive experiences, but the feedback arrives too soon and the instruction arrives too late. We learn, but the sequence does harm.

Яapid readeR

- Instructional design is the process of arranging for learning to happen safely, certainly, thoroughly, and expeditiously.

- Education and training both target successful behavior and can use the same systematic design approach.

- An eclectic design approach is needed, drawing from research, theory, and experience.

While in some ways we probably learn best by direct experience, it's not always possible or desirable to arrange. We can't have doctors developing their skills from the start by experimenting on patients. Nor can we let teenagers go out on the freeways by themselves to learn to drive.

Even when it is possible to learn through direct experience, without guidance, it's often both an inefficient way to gain skills and it provides incomplete knowledge. One might learn how to fly a plane through direct experience, for example. Given that the learner survived, it would take a very long time to become familiar with all the instruments and controls through experimentation. And after all that learning effort, the novice pilot would still be unprepared to deal with emergency situations that had not come up by chance.

The design challenge

Instructional design is simply defined as the process of arranging for learning to happen more safely, certainly, thoroughly, and expeditiously than might otherwise happen. The challenges that belie instructional design are not as genial as the definition may suggest. Over centuries and many civilizations, man has taken many approaches to sharing experiences and transferring skills, almost always discovering more questions than answers. The art of instruction, based on intuition and talent, has been mastered by many consummate teachers, but has been difficult to pass on to others. The science of instruction, based on controlled research, has provided many useful principles but has also awakened us to the vast gaps in our knowledge of how people learn.

Learning is an inherently personal process. No one can learn for us; we cannot learn for our students. But we clearly can facilitate the learning process such that learners require less time, incur less risk, and invest less energy than those who learned from the raw world without assistance. Whether learners learning with our help learn what is true, become proficient, and have as much or more pleasure in the process as we did are true measures of our work.

Whether learners assisted by our designs develop the ability and interest to continue learning, either with or without assistance, is also of importance—at least to designers of educational programs. It's perhaps the most important goal of all, or should be, at least for our schools, but in making structured learning nearly effortless, as we often try to do, we risk depriving learners of the skills for making sense of, and coping with, an unmapped, ever-changing world and the joy of learning that comes from successes. Serving as a bus driver for learners, instructional designers can port learners safely and comfortably to places of popularized interest. But unless an effort is also made to help learners discover the endless unseen miracles that lie in wait along rarely traversed paths, they may end up dependent on tour guides and unable to navigate on their own, let alone devise personally rewarding adventures.

Instructional design is easy to define, but always challenging, even to the most talented and experienced. And now in the information society, with much more content to learn than ever before, and rapidly advancing technologies to channel, design appears to be floundering. Instead of the dynamic, highly personalized learning experiences today's technology enables, we're seeing a dominance of impersonal, content-focused, pseudo-interactive,

and boring presentations. Perhaps it's time to recast our approach.

The big questions

This chapter pursues some big questions prevalent in the minds and literature of today's instructional designers and learning researchers:

➤ What changes to the instructional design process are required, if any, in a communications-rich world influenced by the Internet and rapid knowledge change?

➤ Can a systematic process enable instructional designers to succeed? What are the issues? Most importantly, how does one learn to be a great designer?

➤ Is instructional design an art or science?

➤ Are different processes needed for education and training?

➤ Is the goal of instruction knowledge or performance?

➤ What design approaches are most effective?

Following discussion of these questions, in the next chapter we will turn to *Success-based design*, an eclectic approach so named because of the applied success many have had with it, including my colleagues and myself over hundreds and hundreds of projects. Success-based design is pragmatic and yet enjoys support from research, theory, and consistency with many of the approaches advocated by others. In subsequent chapters, we will review details of this approach and also identify the major points of coherence it has with major design theories.

New challenges

In dramatic, and seemingly sudden contrast to the recent past, communication media are more capable, knowledge is more expansive, and sources of information are more accessible. While the goal of instructional design has been and remains the induction of learning, neither the tools nor expectations have remained the same. Some of these changes are obvious, such as the affordability of distributing video information, the ability to animate illustrations, recognition of spoken commands, and communication with mobile devices. These new capabilities redefine the playing field in both exciting and perplexing ways.

Technology-enriched cultures behave differently from those without easy access to information. Indeed, we ourselves behave differently than we did only a decade or two ago. For example, in our technology-saturated environment, we now not only assume that desired information is freely available, we also expect it to be accessible quickly and easily. If one source of information fails to readily provide what we want, we jump—we search another source, perhaps unwittingly settling for inferior content in the process, but we satisfy our need for speed, for instant gratification. We're actually insulted if even a free source of information serves it up slowly. Similarly, if we are not instantly engaged with an electronic presentation, find it lackluster, or find it poorly tailored to our needs, we search elsewhere or abandon the interest and pursue something else. Mass ADD? It seems so. (I wonder what we'll evolve to next.)

A great deal of thought and investment goes into the creation of successful learning applications. To succeed, designers must deal not only with the innate complexity of the human mind, but also with contemporary behaviors, needs, and expectations that bias perceptions, determine focus, and selectively energize actions. When one is fully aware of all the challenges to be met and risks to be managed, it is clear that design of instructional products is anything but easy. Those unaware of the challenges and risks may delight in the many decidedly enjoyable and creative aspects of the work, but often and unknowingly plant the seeds of instructional failure and lost opportunities. Examples are everywhere.

Systematic process

When people speak of instructional design, they are often referring to systematic approaches—methodical, orderly processes that are believed to produce better learning designs than would be achieved without them. The range of issues considered; the theory, rationale, or experience behind the process; and how they deal with specific issues differentiates instructional design approaches.

In general, we look to every instructional design to specify the following critical attributes of learning interventions:

➤ What happens when (sequence/branching/event selection)
➤ What communication media will be used and for what

➤ Selection and format of information to be presented or made available on request
➤ Learner guidance and conditions under which it will be provided
➤ Performance feedback
➤ How learners will practice what they're learning
➤ Extent of practice required
➤ Means of measuring proficiency
➤ Criteria for completion or mastery

Many systematic approaches have been advanced and used with success [see Resources below for a sampling], yet much of today's e-learning suffers from ineffectiveness. It's clearly possible to do everything "right" according

Resources

📖 **ADDIE Model** Carliner, S. (2003). *Training Design Basics* (ASTD Training Basics). Alexandria, Virginia: American Society for Training & Development.

📖 **Dick and Carey Model** Dick, W., & Carey, L. (1996). *The Systematic Design of Instruction* (4th ed.). New York: Harper Collins College Publishers.

Resources

📖 **Gerlach-Ely Model** Gerlach, U.S. and Ely, D.P. (1980). *Teaching and Media: A Systematic Approach* (2nd ed.). Englewood Cliffs, NJ: Prentice-Hall Incorporated.

📖 **Hannafin-Peck Model** Hannafin, M. J. and Peck, K. L. (1988). *The Design, Development, and Evaluation of Instructional Software.* New York: MacMillan Publishing Company.

📖 **Kemp Model** Kemp, J. (1985). *The instructional design process.* New York: Harper & Row.

📖 **Rapid Prototyping Model** Tripp, S. and Bichelmeyer, B. (1990). Rapid prototyping: An alternative instructional design strategy. *Educational Technology Research & Development, 38*(1), 31 – 44.

---

to many models and still produce inadequate outcomes.

Art or science?

Although there is some evidence that systematic approaches are helpful in the production of higher quality learning designs, we have little comparative evidence for ranking one system over another (Hackbarth, 1996; Gustafson and Branch, 2002; Alessi and Trollip, 2001).

Some believe that instructional design is more truly an art than a science, suggesting that systematic approaches will never achieve the quality that an artist can. Perhaps this view forms from recognizing the creativity needed to engage learners, hold their interest, and deal with the mysteries of human thinking and behavior. Indeed, most models are much more at home in discussion of cognitive issues than affective ones, while design artisans sometimes achieve a much more effective balance.

Some critics actually oppose any attempts at systematic design (Damarin, 1994), fearing that if they were highly effective, instructional interventions would tyrannically entrap minds and shape behaviors against the learner's will. But this extreme position ultimately argues against any effective learning programs, regardless of how they were crafted, systematically or otherwise.

We are far from possessing the ability to create e-learning programs that oppress minds and suppress voluntary behavior (although we certainly have demonstrated many ways to victimize learners and torture them with boredom). What we're searching for today are procedures for designing learning applications that can be built within realistic constraints of time and resources and

Resources

📖 Alessi, S. and Trollip, S. (2001). *Multimedia for Learning: Methods and Development*, (3rd ed.) Needham Heights, MA: Allyn & Bacon.

📖 Damarin, S. (1994). Equity, caring, and beyond: Can feminist ethics inform educational technology? *Educational Technology, 34*, p. 37.

📖 Gustafson, K. L. and Branch, R. M. (2002). *Survey of Instructional Design Models* (4th ed.). Syracuse, NY: ERIC Clearinghouse on Information.

📖 Hackbarth, S. (1996). *The Educational Technology Handbook: A Comprehensive Guide to Process and Products for Learning.* Englewood Cliffs, NJ: Educational Technology Publications. (p. 58)

that do interest and enable learners in behaving more effectively.

Clearly, there's value in having a process to help with the complexity and enormity of the instructional design task, even for the most talented designers. There's value in experimental studies that show varying outcomes attributable to different instructional designs. And there is value in having considerable experience as a designer. Even with the most prescriptive approaches available today, outcomes will vary with the talent and inventiveness of the designer. Conversely, even great designers can fail to produce effective applications without the aid of a systematic approach, especially when large projects are undertaken. There's simply too much challenge for most designers to succeed without the aid of process.

Art or science? Perhaps instructional design should be called a *craft*—a blend of science and art—but regardless of semantics, good instructional design benefits from both. The sciences of human learning and educational psychology identify issues of concern, suggest approaches that have been successful under carefully identified conditions, and provide the means to evaluate the appropriateness of design choices. Creativity is needed to adapt to specific needs and circumstances, fill in the many gaps between substantiated principles, and provide the aesthetics, drama, tension, and humor needed to entice learner participation. Both art and science are invaluable to making learning happen, and it's apparent when one is missing.

Education versus training

Is the same instructional design process fitting for both education and training? Are different approaches better for one than the other?

One expects to find stark contrasts between education and training, perhaps because we see them happening in different venues. Education happens in schoolrooms and at home. Training happens in corporations, the military, sports, and athletics. Given these contexts, we chain our thoughts forward to think education is somehow softer, more accommodating, and interested in producing well-rounded individuals who can cope effectively with both expected and unforeseen challenges. Training, on the other hand, is focused on specifically defined tasks. It's no nonsense, hard, and demanding. Efficiency is paramount. The purpose of training is to develop specific skills, as fast as possible, to deal with specific tasks.

This perspective is too neat and simple to be right, isn't it? Let's examine a few contradictions: We *train* elementary school children on basic math, writing, and comprehension skills (or at least we used to). These are basic intellectual skills everyone is likely to find valuable. Adherence to standards is often prerequisite: *He and I are going..., Not, Him and I are going....* Conversely, we prepare business managers to solve problems, listen effectively, and provide leadership (or at least we ought to). People need to have these skills for dealing with life's broad range of daily challenges and opportunities. In both schools and training environments, successful performance at all levels requires having generalized knowledge and specific skills, and it's *all* the province of instructional design.

Effective instructional design approaches must therefore provide assistance in developing both specific skills and generalized cognitive skills for inventing, evaluating, coping, and enjoying life. Although different instructional events may be appropriate for different outcomes, we shouldn't have to look for different design approaches. A robust, systematic approach should identify what is needed and provide matching heuristics.

Education vs. Training

Knowing versus doing

The education versus training debate is sometimes reframed as a knowing versus doing debate. From this perspective, education is focused on *acquisition* of knowledge while training is focused on *application* of knowledge; in other words, education is about *knowing* and training is about *doing*.

From the training perspective, it's easy to see that no retailer, swim coach, or army general will be satisfied if his people can correctly answer multiple-choice questions about performing their assigned tasks but fumble in the process of performing them. Successes come from people actually doing the right things at the right times, not from only knowing what should be done.

Do educators care only about knowing? Of course not. Well, perhaps some do. I knew some of them. Just like TV game show hosts, I had some history teachers who felt their jobs were to teach us to recall the dates of events, the names of military and political leaders, nomenclature for social classes, and so on. All with little context and no purpose. I hated it. And I forgot almost everything they tried to drill into me.

Much later, a college friend decided to major in history education. I thought he was out of his mind for choosing something so boring. But then he corrected my misconceptions by showing me that history is and can be taught as a tool for evaluating current events, creating strategies and social programs, creating multinational trade agreements, and generally making sense of things otherwise appearing senseless. The classes he taught were fun, exciting, mesmerizing—you could see it in the faces of his young students as they blasted into his school room, eager to find what was in store for them. You could *do* something with history. No, not boring. Empowering. It wasn't just about knowing.

Educational organizations really are in the business of helping learners become capable performers, even if the outcome performance is simply the ability to carry on an intelligent conversation about art, enjoy a musical performance, or vote with rationality. And while training

Knowing vs. Doing

events are obviously about producing outcome performances, they are also concerned with instilling knowledge. Trainers see knowledge, just as good educators do, as an important enabler of performance. They know that people who understand not only the *whens* and *hows* of performance, but also the *whys—Why is this action preferred? Why does inaction cause problems?*—can be better performers, adapt to changing situations, and feel more satisfied by their contributions.

In the end, training and education are not differentiated by an exclusive interest in either knowledge or performance; rather, they each share the purpose of enhancing both. Education is, perhaps, focused on broader areas of outcome performance abilities where training typically has a more narrow focus, but we do not otherwise find differences in either desired outcomes or appropriate designs to stimulate learning.

We bother with these reflections in order to determine whether differentiated design methods are needed or whether one approach can reasonably serve both education and training. I conclude that one design approach fits the needs of both while recognizing that some differences in the final product may be appropriate. Training programs may, for example, be effective with a narrower set of application exercises, but justify a higher level of over learning. *Trainees will learn which of our insurance policies are appropriate for financially independent retirees and be able to identify their pros and cons instantly in a sales conversation.* Exercises in an educational program may need to be broader. *Learners will identify the characteristics of insurance policies that determine suitability for financially independent retirees.*

Ultimately, both education and training need programs that enhance learner motivation, provide behavior-enhancing learning experiences, and make those experiences meaningful and memorable—all with the intent of achieving excellent performance.

Alternative design approaches

Approaches to instructional design can be classified as intuitive, research-based, theory-based, and success-based.

What training-related practices might improve education? What education-related practices might improve training?

Think

Intuitive approaches

Due to the rapid adoption of e-learning, promulgated by the Internet and the ubiquity of media-enabled computers, the large majority of people serving as instructional designers has little formal schooling in instructional design. Lack of formal preparation doesn't mean one is necessarily a poor instructional designer. Quite the contrary, unschooled people have created some of the best instructional designs I've seen, whereas proud, confident, degree- and certificate-bedecked designers have conjured some of the worst designs ever foisted upon innocent learners. And vice versa.

Some public speakers can mesmerize an audience. They do so with an intuitive sense of timing, sequencing, and intonation. The most successful recognize not only their inborn talent but also attribute much to extensive practice. At one point in his life, Jay Leno worked 300 clubs a year! He still *practices for hours* before every show. He's often the first "Tonight Show" employee to arrive for work and the last to leave.

Some instructional designers have found inborn talent. Perhaps through keen awareness of their own learning needs, successes, and failures, they were able to derive and apply guiding principles that work. The unfortunate reality of today, however, is that the powerful interactive multimedia and communications resources available to support learning are often inappropriately and ineffectively employed because of poor instructional design. Too many people are working unguided by knowledge and experience in what is truly challenging work.

Just as corporations initially underestimated the cost and difficulty of designing and supporting competitive websites for promotion and sale of their products by multiple levels of magnitude, they have also tended to underestimate the importance of designing online learning well. People with neither an intuitive sense for good design nor acquired design skills are often responsible for designing today's e-learning applications. Disappointingly, many of these poorly designed applications are delivered to large numbers of learners with destructive consequences ranging from an enormous waste of human time to incompetent performance in hazardous situations.

Which one of the following objectives will be your organization's highest e-learning priority in 2006? (Select only one)

33% Improve the quality of e-learning content

21% Extend the global reach of the e-learning content

| 0% | 10% | 20% | 30% | 40% | 50% | 60% | 70% | 80% | 90% | 100% |

The top two priorities selected by respondents to e-Learning Guild's surveys reflect concerns about content and design (Pulichini, 2006).

Resources

🖥 elearningguild.com The e-Learning Guild maintains a continually updated online library of survey studies and other helpful white papers.

📖 Gartner. (2005). Client issues in the high-performance workplace. ID Number G00126793. Cited in Boehle, S. Sept. 2005, The state of the e-learning market. *Training*, pp. 12-18.

🖥 Pulichino, J. (2006). Future Directions in e-Learning Research Report 2006. Downloaded from www.elearningguild.com/research/archives.

Surveys [see Resources below] are indicating that organizations, many of which initially underestimated the importance of quality design and what it takes to achieve it, are learning. Quality design has become one of the most important success factors and goals of these organizations. The e-Learning Guild's 2005 and 2006 surveys, for example, both found one-third of respondents selecting "Improve the quality of e-learning content" as their highest priority (Pulichino, 2006, p. 7). According to Gartner research, "High-quality content is the most important factor used to determine the success of e-learning efforts" (Gartner, 2005).

Although intuitive approaches occasionally succeed, the costs of wasted learner time, missed opportunities, and poor performance require reliable, replicable approaches that achieve success every time. We do have to have enough knowledge and experience to make success through other approaches, if not a certainty, at least a very high probability.

Research-based approaches

Research on human learning and on the comparative effects of alternative instructional designs has been going on for a very long time, and we know quite a bit about both. Knowledge of stimulus-response relationships provide helpful guidance for instructional and user interface design, for example. Practice leads to increased performance ability. Distributing learning events so they are spaced over time is powerful, although it is rarely done in instructional designs. Comprehension of on-screen text is measurably lower than comprehension of printed text. And so on (see sidebar).

However, and with respect for scientific research second to none, I must suggest that research has not provided an effective rudder for many instructional designers. Whether this is primarily because research is difficult to interpret and apply properly, because research principles are too narrow for general application, or because designers are unaware of applicable research is, I suppose, arguable. No doubt all of these factors come into play.

With increasing realization that much of today's e-learning is poorly designed and responding to "proven guidelines" unabashedly touted with increasing frequency (many of which are quite over-generalized), research-based instructional design has drawn some recent attention. While many of us have hoped for decades to see design based more firmly on research, many intuitive

Notes on Human Learning
by distinguished learning researcher and founding director of the Talaris Research Institute, John Medina*

➢ Human brains do not receive and process information like "video tape recorders." They deconstruct input, and then reconstruct meaning.

➢ Every brain is wired differently from every other brain, individually processing information in ways unique to that wiring.

➢ People are natural explorers, using hypothesis testing to process information. This tendency can be observed in early infancy and is probably genetic.

➢ Practice increases learning. Repetition and rehearsal are critical for the successful creation of long-term memories.

➢ Half of the human brain cortex is devoted to processing visual information. We process visual information more effectively than any other type.

➢ Focused attentional states facilitate learning. The maintenance of such states may be directly proportional to the emotional content of the subject.

➢ People do not learn optimally from continuous, long stretches of linearly supplied information. Deliberate ... breaks ... critical for comprehension.

➢ Stressed brains do not learn the same way as non-stressed brains.

---

*Presented at the Embry-Riddle Aeronautical University Symposium, 2001

designers are now putting stock in glibly promoted principles that have validity only in specific circumstances—a restriction that is easily overlooked when there is pressure to complete designs and generate learning applications quickly.

Spurring on responsibility-laden designers are those who, too eagerly, in this author's view, over-generalize research findings and offer them as dependable directives, implying applicability that is often far from proven. On close examination, some popularized "research-based" guidelines fall far outside what the research actually reveals and is sometimes even contrary to outcomes actually and frequently observed. It's not the research studies or results that are concerning, it's the design principles derived from them that give us pause.

This criticism is not directed to researchers, as researchers tend to be extraordinarily reluctant to generalize outside the precise framework in which their experimental results were derived. It does often work to go beyond what is proven, but extrapolation is chancy and should be recognized as such with proper warning and qualification.

Although I frequently see new designers oversimplifying the problems their designs must address and, simultaneously, improvising designs with little recognition of applicable research, Driscoll and Carliner

(2005) point out that new designers tend to cling closely to research as a guide because they lack experience to draw upon. Driscoll and Carliner advise, most astutely, that "What new designers have to realize, however, is that the more different the situation they face is from the one described in the research study, the less they can rely on that study to predict the likelihood of their own success" (p. 20). Even understanding this, as surely most designers do, it's difficult to determine what situational differences are likely to have an impact; ever more so for inexperienced designers.

Perhaps the most responsible application of a research-based approach is looking to research to suggest designs for consideration, realizing that any one of many possible differences between the researcher's setting and one's own may invalidate the research applicability. Any source of intuitively appealing designs has value in a process that Driscoll and Carliner properly describe as problem solving. It is critical, however, that design decisions actually be evaluated in the process. Indeed, the successive approximation process we use in this book series promotes early experimentation with multiple designs and with actual learners to determine what works before the design is finalized and fully developed.

Resources
📖 Driscoll, M. and Carliner, S. (2005). *Advanced Web-Based Training Strategies: Unlocking Instructionally Sound Online Learning.* San Francisco: Pfeiffer.

💻 Thalheimer, W. (2006). Spacing learning events over time: What the research says. Retrieved Dec. 15, 2006, from http://www.work-learning. com/catalog/

Considering the complexity and uniqueness of each attempt to develop desired behaviors, clarity of thought and objectivity throughout the process are the most apt and constantly desired companions followed by a healthy knowledge of research methods and findings.

Theory-based approaches
Theorists recognize that research findings are often incomplete and inadequate to guide complex practices, that without a context for the knowledge we have and a perspective for interpretation, research findings can and do cause technicians to make dreadful mistakes, even though each decision taken in isolation may appear to be supported by research.

Theories are developed to 1) provide explanations for findings, 2) fill in the blanks between established facts, 3) predict outcomes not yet researched, and 4) suggest research that is needed. Theories for instructional design do exist, if in somewhat ragtag forms, and they can provide helpful guidance to instructional designers.

For an overview perspective, most, if not all, of today's theoretical design approaches can be seen as derivatives of behaviorist, cognitivist, and constructivist viewpoints.

Behaviorism
Applying the principles of learning and behavioral conditioning developed by Edward Thorndike, John Watson (who coined the term *behaviorism*), and B.F. Skinner, Gagné set the foundations of modern instructional design. "Extrapolating beyond the evidence...[Gagné] produced a formal framework to guide teaching practice. This 'creative leap' made by Gagné provided the basis for the subsequent development of

instructional design. In the view of its critics it also provides its central weakness" (Boyle, 1997, p. 68).

Behaviorists take a relatively simple view of learning. Based on the notion of operant conditioning—behaviors that are rewarded tend to be exhibited more often than those that aren't—we can teach by having learners practice and by giving positive rewards for correct responses. Knowledge of results is often found to be a sufficient reward. Whether learners actually understand why their responses are correct is not of great concern as long as learners respond correctly.

There's no doubt that the rationale, principles, and techniques set forth by behaviorists have had great influence. I suspect that the evolution of my own thinking about instructional design parallels that of many of my contemporaries who also began their careers adhering closely to behavioristic principles and have become less and less satisfied with the results. Because the process is really an attempt to implant improved performance, and little effort is made to build a

network of understanding, learners have trouble responding to new situations, creating new responses or adapting old ones, and reaping satisfaction from applying intelligence during the learning process. These are major weaknesses not to be overlooked.

Perhaps worse, although behavioristic principles are the most widely known principles for instructional design, they tend to produce boring learning events, especially for adult learners. They put cognitive blinders on learners as if they were horses, unable to cope with real world stimuli. As Alessi and Trollip (2001) so aptly put it:

A strict behavioral approach, paying attention only to observable learner behaviors and ways to influence them, is not appropriate for multimedia design (p. 36). We believe the strict Instructional Systems Design (ISD) method that grew out of the behavioral approach resulted in much instructional software that was dry, unmotivating, and difficult to apply in new situations (p. 37).

While most designers today eschew behaviorism in discussion, there's no doubt that these principles still guide much of their thinking. Happily, if the needed outcome is more of a rapid reflex than a thoughtful response, behavioristic techniques are probably just the ticket. But behaviorism is clearly not a sufficient and comprehensive guide for e-learning design. We need to get out of the Skinner box if e-learning is going to realize its potential.

Cognitivism

Human behavior is surprisingly unpredictable if your only view of learning and behavior is from a behavioristic viewpoint. It's hard, for example, to explain successful behaviors that have never been explicitly learned (practiced and reinforced). Something else is going on in our brains besides stimulus and response linkages.

Cognitivists, while recognizing that reinforcement does affect the probability of certain behaviors, are interested in modeling the mental structures and processes that seem necessary to more fully explain human behavior. If we can devise accurate models, we can then create learning events to address more complex behaviors, such as problem solving.

Note: Gagné didn't confine his thinking to behaviorism, as many critics contend. He actually assumed that different types of instructional approaches are appropriate for different types of learning. He continued his work (Gagné and Medsker, 1995), giving consideration to factors that affect adult learning, and synthesizing cognitivist views.

There are many useful constructs in cognitivism to guide instructional design, such as *organization*—noting that information is easier to remember if it is structured or has a context, *meaning*—noting that it is easier to recall information if it is linked to many things already understood and anchored in memory, and *schema*—noting that we compare structures of information and concepts (think of analogies), not just points of fact, and that we can learn new information more easily if it is similar to existing schema.

Cognitivists see learning as a willful activity, requiring attention and energy. As a result, issues of perception, techniques of gathering learner attention, and motivating learners are central and provide an excellent basis for e-learning design work, ranging from user-interface and display design to techniques to motivate learners and sequence content.

We will see these concepts, added to the useful concepts of behaviorism and constructivism, surfacing in success-based design discussed in the next chapter and throughout much of this book.

Constructivism

Constructivists theorize that we cannot ingest knowledge, understanding, and skills. We need to construct our own representations of the world and how things work. If we predigest knowledge for our learners, spitting it out in small, tender bites, as designers often do in an effort to make learning easier, we deprive learners of an essential learning activity. Learners actually need to put everything back together and then take it apart for themselves. Put another way, while we can recount experiences for learners and have them regurgitate them, they learn at a much more superficial level than if they could have those experiences themselves.

Jonassen, et al. (1999) list constructivist assumptions about learning, including the following (pp. 3-5):

➢ Constructivists believe that knowledge is constructed, not transmitted.

➢ Knowledge construction results from activity, so knowledge is embedded in activity.

➢ Knowledge is anchored in and indexed by the context in which the learning activity occurs.

➢ Meaning is in the mind of the knower.

➢ Meaning making is prompted by a problem, question, confusion, disagreement, or dissonance (a need or desire to know) and so involves personal ownership of that problem.

Minimalism is an instructional technique based on constructivist principles that has had significant success in application (Carroll, 1998). John Carroll coined the name after observing that many instructional designs were at extreme odds with the way adults like to learn:

People want to learn by doing, but this inclines them to jump around opportunistically in learning sequences. They want to reason things out and construct their own understandings, but they are not always planful, and they often draw incorrect inferences. They try to engage and extend their prior knowledge and skill, but this can lead to interference or over-generalization. They try to learn through error diagnosis and recovery, but errors can be subtle, can tangle, and can become intractable obstacles to comprehension and motivation (p. 6).

These observations are something of a wake-up call to many designers, who have had similar observations and wish learners would just behave. A more constructive response (the pun is nice) is to restructure learning events to meet the natural desires of learners. Minimalism responds with the design principles paraphrased from van der Meij and Carroll (1998, pp. 19-53) below:

1. Choose an action-oriented approach. Get learners doing things as soon as possible, support exploration, and provide helpful, respectful feedback.

2. Anchor activities in the task domain. Provide authentic tasks for learners to perform, making sure not to overwhelm novices while giving advanced learners something of interest and value.

3. Support error recognition and recovery. Provide tools to help learners discover their mistakes and make corrections.

4. Use text to help learners perform, study, and locate help.

Keep text very brief, don't explain everything, and make each reference item independent so that learners don't have to search for meaningful answers.

Resources

📖 Alessi, S. and Trollip, S. (2001). *Multimedia for Learning: Methods and Development*, (3rd ed.) Needham Heights, MA: Allyn & Bacon.

📖 Boyle, T. (1997). *Design for Multimedia Learning*. Essex, England: Prentice Hall.

📖 Carroll, J.M. (Ed.) (1998). *Minimalism Beyond the Nurnberg Funnel*. Cambridge, MA: MIT Press.

📖 Gagné, R.M. and Medsker, K.L. (1995) *The Conditions of Learning: Training Applications*. Belmont, CA: Wadsworth Publishing.

📖 Jonassen, D.H., Peck, K.L., and Wilson, B.G. (1999). *Learning with technology: A Constructivist Perspective*. Upper Saddle River, NJ: Prentice Hall.

📖 van der Meij, H. and Carroll, J.M. (1998). Principles and heuristics for designing minimalist instruction. *Minimalism Beyond the Nurnberg Funnel*. J.M. Carroll. (Ed.). Cambridge, MA: MIT Press.

I'll take all three

Each of these three theory-based approaches has appealing aspects, and there is no reason why designers need to work exclusively in one. Indeed, experienced designers tend to switch from one approach to another as the case warrants. The choice should be made based first on research findings, if they are available and applicable. If no formal, relevant evidence exists, then observed success should guide the choice. And if that's not available, then careful conjecture.

In the following chapter, we'll pick up success-based design. It is a blend of approaches that has led to consistently high levels of success. As one researcher put it, "It's amazing how the principles of success-based design are increasingly substantiated by research and consistent with newer theoretical positions." There's nothing like consistent success to draw attention and consideration!

Summary

Although the world is instructive, we can speed the sharing of knowledge and the development of skills through well-designed learning events. Talented people can sometimes develop effective learning experiences through intuitive means, but lacking extraordinary talent and also a basis for effective instructional design, many of today's designers are missing the mark.

Most designers need well-defined guiding principles on which to base their decisions. Because education and training are ultimately interested in enabling performance, the same processes can serve them both.

Alternative systematic processes include research-based, theory-based, and success-based approaches. This chapter reviews the first two, while the latter is the subject of the next chapter.

Research-based approaches can provide the strongest specific guidance, but the error of over-generalization is common, leading to poor designs. Theory-based approaches provide more practical guidance while recognizing that some tenets are conjectural. The primary theory-based approaches are behaviorism, cognitivism, and constructivism. While the strongest advocates of an approach may be critical of the others, most practitioners today find use for all three approaches.

6 | Success-Based Design

"If you try to fail, and succeed, which have you done?"

Thinking? OK, how about this one: "If at first you don't succeed, redefine success." I chuckle at these jokes, but also wince a bit when I realize how close to home they hit.

Some designs seem like overt attempts to fail—they certainly aren't going to result in performance improvements. And how do they measure their "success"? They produce lovely posttest scores and smile sheets. But that's not success.

Listening to some one-liners today helped me view instructional design from a lighter perspective. You see, I think it's almost criminal each and every time a boring, ineffective e-learning application is foisted on learners. The wasted time, the negative backlash on the golden potential of e-learning,

the effects of poor performance, the frustration! Painful. And yet, we push forward and, I suppose, I get too serious about it all.

"If at first you don't succeed, skydiving definitely isn't for you!" But instructional design? You can manage. With lessons garnered from successful projects and designers to guide you, you can succeed, even in your first attempt. "Always remember, you're unique (just like everyone else)." You'll develop your own style. There isn't just one right way to design successful e-learning. "I couldn't repair your brakes, so I made your horn louder." Rim shot.

Making good decisions

Let's get directly to the issue: What do we really need to do to be successful designers?

It's not learning to know the history of instructional design. Knowing and doing are quite different things. It's not really being able to recall the history of instructional design either; that won't ensure design success.

It's not to compare and contrast theories. Knowledge of theories doesn't mean you know how to create successful learning programs.

It's not to cite research on human learning or the lineage of instructional practice. These skills won't get a course designed.

No, successful designers create behavior-changing experiences. Period. They alternatively look at the details of possible learning solutions and at the big picture. They try as soon as possible to identify the pivotal issues in each circumstance and at each level of the design, knowing that every situation is unique in some ways.

What would be your terminal objectives for an instructional program on instructional design?

Think

Although many points of knowledge come to the aid of an instructional designer, designers succeed only when their work leads learners to successful performance. And that's what successful designers do.

Again, what do we really need to do to be successful designers? Make a long string of good decisions. And just as it's better practice to study the language you really want to speak, rather than studying Latin to prepare yourself to learn another language, instructional designers need to focus directly on design decisions. There are plenty of issues here to challenge anyone, and yet the process is often made needlessly complicated or over-simplified. Success lies between these extremes.

In this chapter, we begin with some fundamental principles of success-based design. The fundamental principles are few in number, helping designers keep the focus where it needs to be and avoid becoming overwhelmed with a task that can otherwise become overwhelming.

Thinking helps

I've extolled using a systematic approach. There's no question it helps. But no approach, no matter how systematic and detailed, will lead designers to success if they abdicate good reasoning, forgo iterative evaluation, and follow a cookbook. I've had graduate students bring me designs that were, frankly, abominable. Most, mind you, present wonderfully inventive designs. I'm usually on cloud nine at the end of a term. But sometimes.... Awful.

When I ask students why they did something misguided, the response is almost always grounded in a valid principle. If I comment, for example, *that decision made your interactions very confusing for learners,* I'll inevitably get the response, *I thought so too!* Huh? That's why I'm so adamant about "forgetting what you 'know' about instructional design and doing something interesting." If it isn't interesting, doesn't have appeal to learners, doesn't have them practicing authentic skills, doesn't help them build an understanding of how good performance is beneficial, then it's not good. Many of these characteristics are pretty obvious, and designers need to be awake, evaluating, and thinking, not just doing.

Of course, the principles novice designers base their poor decisions on probably do not recommend the decisions they make. A superficial understanding of principles leads easily to poor design. And that's unfortunately what we have too much of today: superficial understanding of important principles. And, if I may, a willingness to disregard our common sense and gut reactions. If you wouldn't want to learn through an application of your design, your learners probably won't want to either.

Don't forget to step back and ask yourself: Would you want to spend your learning time in the way you've prescribed—and do you think you would learn from it? Forget how much work you put into the design, how hard it was to come up with it, and how hard it was to get acceptance by the stakeholders. If it grates (or numbs) the senses, it's bad.

The best of everything

Success-based design is an amalgamation of approaches, theories, research, and experience, and, as we saw in the previous book in this series, it is systematic. It is also pragmatic, settling for what works best for the learner, regardless of theoretical bias or consistency. It uses the designer's time and resources wisely, and it focuses on those things that matter most in application—where learners are often under a myriad of pressures, expectations, and distractions and where learning may not be the learner's first order of interest.

In the previous chapter we reviewed three theoretical approaches, behaviorism, cognitivism, and constructivism. Although the advocates of one are sometimes critical of the others, the masterful designers I've had opportunities to work with easily incorporate the perspectives and techniques of two or all three in their designs.

Ertmer and Newby (1993) propose an interesting means of selecting theoretical approaches based on two factors: the learner's level of task knowledge and the level of cognitive processing required by the task. With respect to the learner's knowledge, "...a behavioral approach can effectively facilitate mastery of the content...(knowing what); cognitive strategies are useful in teaching problem-solving tactics where defined facts and rules are applied in unfamiliar situations (knowing how); and constructivist strategies are especially suited to dealing with ill-defined problems through reflection-in-action."

The level of cognitive processing required also affects which strategy is likely to succeed. "For example, tasks requiring a low degree of processing (e.g., basic paired associations, discriminations, rote memorization) seem to be facilitated by strategies most frequently associated with a behavioral outlook (e.g., stimulus-response, contiguity of feedback/ reinforcement). Tasks requiring an increased level of processing (e.g., classifications, rule or procedural executions) are primarily associated with strategies having a stronger cognitive emphasis (e.g., schematic organization, analogical reasoning, algorithmic problem solving). Tasks demanding high levels of processing (e.g., heuristic problem solving, personal selection, and monitoring of cognitive strategies) are frequently best learned with strategies advanced by the constructivist perspective (e.g., situated learning, cognitive apprenticeships, social negotiation)."

Selection of these recommended strategies often comes naturally from the principles of success-based design and in concert with the arguments of Ertmer and Newby simply through efforts to make learning events meaningful, memorable, and motivational for

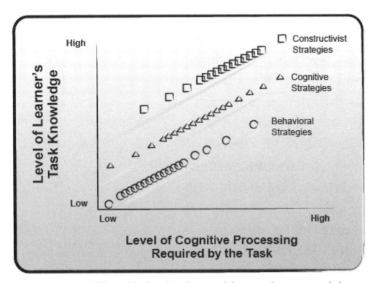

Applicability of behavioral, cognitive, and constructivist instructional strategies (Ertmer and Newby, 1993)

Resource

📖 Ertmer, P.A. and Newby, T.J. (1993). Behaviorism, cognitivism, constructivism: Comparing critical features from an instructional design perspective. *Performance Improvement Quarterly*, 6(4), 50-70. Figure reproduced with permission of the authors and publisher.

an identified learner population. Further, it often happens that strategies are intertwined, such as when a learner opts to tackle a problem a bit beyond his or her ability. A problem-solving exercise (constructivist exercise) might be put on hold while the learner practices some more basic skills (behaviorist exercise).

With this, we're looking ahead a bit, just to note that success-based design is not particularly concerned with theoretical purity, and also to note that theoretical perspectives continue to arise in support of what success-based designers are doing in practice. Sometimes theory leads practice, sometimes the reverse. Whichever is in front, it's clear that success-based design is very much supported by contemporary theories and vice versa.

Watch where you step

Success-based design begins with a reluctance to see instruction as the solution, because achieving behavioral change through learning is not easy. Other solutions may be far more effective and also less expensive. *Are necessary tools available, do performers know what you want them to do, do they have time to do it, are they rewarded more for doing something else, etc.?* Designers must make sure they're not up against factors controlling behavior that have nothing to do with things that can be taught and learned.

When behavioral change does require the development of new skill or kicking bad habits, then the onus is to launch a program that can have real impact. Getting the framework right determines the outcomes. Success or failure.

For example, an in-depth learning experience might help people remember the detailed attributes of each item in a large product line, but given the possibility of instant online access to this information, it may be far more knowledge than is needed, an impracticality, and a waste of precious learner time. Further, if the product specifications were changed frequently, it would be better for people to check online data to be sure of accuracy than to correctly recall it from personal memory but deliver out of date information.

If a performance problem can be solved by provision of information, then an instructional application is more than is needed and may not, in fact, be very effective (annoying learners isn't usually the best strategy). It is important, therefore, prior to invoking instructional design as a solution, to be sure the problem is one that can and should be solved via training solutions. Be reluctant to step in with a learning program until you know it's the right thing to do.

The three Ms

When designing and developing a learning intervention is an appropriate thing to do, focusing on just three fundamental targets will guide your work and make success a high probability: Make learning experiences M1) meaningful, M2) memorable, and M3) motivational. While there are many relevant issues and controversies in the field of instructional design—more than any full time scholar can master continuously—the 3 Ms focus on the

heart of the matter. Not that they're easy, but putting your attention on these targets and the design issues they raise almost assures a successful design.

M1: Meaningful learning experiences

Does the content make sense to the learner and build on currently held knowledge and skills? Do the expected outcomes have meaning in his or her life? We're looking at individual fit here: What's meaningful to one person isn't necessarily meaningful to another, perhaps because of ability to comprehend, opportunity to use the knowledge, or values held.

A propulsion engineer, for example, might find little meaning in fashion design techniques, although be quite able to understand them. A remote island fisherman might well see the value of geometry skills in his craft, but be unable to comprehend the mathematics without preparatory learning. These are extreme cases to make the point, of course, but design work would be necessary in both to establish the necessary base of meaningfulness.

If the content is not meaningful to the individual, the learner will not be able to assist in the learning process. The learner will have trouble maintaining focus, practicing sufficiently, and being able to apply learning outcomes if any occur. In other words, meaningfulness is the gateway to learning complex skills and is a design prerequisite.

M2: Memorable learning experiences

Learning activities must make a lasting imprint on the learner if behavior subsequent to instruction and posttests is to be improved. Is there sufficient impact, perhaps through imagery, surprise, amazement, practice, or other devices to help learners retain what they've learned? This isn't just about novelty—it's about creating something that the learner will *remember*. For example, is enough practice provided and is it spaced with sufficient breaks between practice sessions that are long enough for new skills to endure? Are learners given useful cognitive structures or, better yet, encouraged to develop and apply their own?

M3: Motivational learning experiences

We have two motivations to be concerned about, and both are critical for success. Learners must have motivation to learn, or they won't, and learners must have motivation to transfer their learning to actual performance, or they won't.

For learning to occur and future behavior to change, learners must expend energy. They won't do this unless they see a reason to do so. Does the instructional design provide motivation-building experiences so that learners will actually complete the instruction, reach the targeted level of performance, and apply the new skills beyond the conclusion of training? Does the design recognize any incentives not to learn or, more likely, not to change current behavior patterns and help learners remove or resist them?

The fourth M: Measurable results

Finally, the acid test: did the intervention yield the targeted performance? Although the 3 Ms provide design direction, they are just the means to the *Big M;* what we really want is measurably improved performance that begets needed results. We're not talking just about posttest scores here, but an authentic ability to perform more effectively after training.

If design work identifies the performance that is actually needed, enables learners to perform at the levels needed, and helps motivate learners to actually perform, then success is at hand. It's a lot, but such is the providence of the instructional designer.

Characteristics of successful designs

In an extremely helpful attempt to identify the "first principles" of instruction and provide a solid foundation for instructional design decisions, noted learning researcher M. David Merrill has set forth an initial set of principles that are consistent with research findings, experience, and multiple design theories. In a very practical manner, Merrill did not try to establish unassailable evidence of validity, but rather assumed "...perhaps without sufficient justification, that if a principle is included in several instructional design theories, the principle has been found either through experience or empirical research to be valid." (Merrill, 2002, p. 44).

None of the theories he reviewed spoke to all proposed principles, but neither did any theory counter the principles he found common. Most theories, however, supported most of the principles, even though terminology varied considerably.

In a similar fashion, William Montague (1988, p. 129) synthesized a set of heuristics for instructional design from principles provided by cognitive scientists (see Table 6.2).

Both the Merrill and Montague principles are consistent with the heuristics my design studios have applied to a wide range of hundreds of e-learning applications with very satisfactory results. Not surprisingly, these first principles provide only part of the guidance designers need, but the guidance they provide is invaluable and we take them into account fully.

It takes an amalgamation of

Resources

📖 Merrill, M.D. (2002). First principles of instruction. *Educational Technology Research and Development, 50*(3). 43-59.

📖 Montague, W.E. (1988). Promoting cognitive processing and learning by designing the learning environment. In D.H. Jonassen (Ed.). *Instructional Designs for Microcomputer Courseware.* Hillsdale, NJ: Lawrence Erlbaum.

Table 6.1 Merrill's First Principles

Principle	Learning is promoted when learners...
Demonstration principle	observe a demonstration.
Application principle	apply the new knowledge.
Task-centered principle	engage in a task-centered instructional activity.
Activation principle	activate prior knowledge or experience.
Integration principle	integrate their new knowledge into their everyday world.

the theories and models currently available, plus some, to provide the broad spectrum of instructional design guidance needed to succeed in real life circumstances. Just as it makes sense to assume validity when a principle is espoused by multiple theories, until proven otherwise, of course, it also makes sense to assume validity when a principle repeatedly leads to success in practice.

Success-based instructional design seems like the smartest approach given what is and isn't known today. It is an eclectic approach, incorporating useful principles

Table 6.2
Montague's Synthesis of Heuristics for Instruction

Use a situational context

Analyze tasks systematically

Provide realistic practice

Minimize memory load initially

Analyze performance errors for causes

Provide corrective feedback

Develop students' self-monitoring skills

from theoretical sources, research, and observed successes, and always keeping eye on the Ms (meaningful, memorable, and motivational learning experiences for measurable results). To provide 1) a useful structure, 2) handy clarity, 3) practical guidance, and 4) evidence of broad-based support, recommendations of the leading theoretical models are aligned with the three design Ms in subsequent chapters.

A practical and realistic guide

My purpose in this book is to help you become a successful e-learning designer who is able to cope with the multiple constraints and challenges designers face in the real world. I hope to help you compromise where compromising will not preclude success, and to help you win support for good design decisions even when your project sponsor initially opposes them. And through it all, I hope to help you develop instructional designs that are spectacularly successful.

Knowing what works and doesn't is important. For the practitioner, it's more important to accurately predict what will and won't work than to actually know why, although

the ability to speak knowledgeably of both is clearly optimal.

Please note that I've taken liberties in extracting and aligning points from various theories, actual projects, and instructional successes of various sorts, sometimes without sharing much justification. I've written this as if I were mentoring an eager but somewhat novice designer in hopes of catapulting him or her to some early successes— successes that would provide firsthand experience upon which to build personal insights and perhaps a life-long career in instructional design.

Nevertheless, as I have worked to compile these guidelines and reviewed them with professional designers, we all feel the organization of concepts put forth here will be of help both to all advanced designers, including ourselves. One really does need a structure to help combat cognitive overload of instructional design.

The real world of design

Few projects have the luxury of being designed in the laboratory, where the prime objective is deeper design insight. Thankfully, some do. In such settings, designers can take their time and explore the comparative impact of alternate designs. A designer may not have to gather any group consensus to take a direction of personal interest and see where it leads.

This guide is constructed primarily for professional designers who typically contend with many constraints and must compromise design decisions when they know that such compromises will also compromise results.

In the rapid prototyping venue (detailed in *Creating Successful e-Learning*—the first book of this library), the designer creates initial solutions in discussion and collaboration with others. Few, if any, of the participants in that setting, other than the instructional designer, are likely to have well-rounded instructional design knowledge and skills, but all are likely to have opinions, sometimes strong opinions, about instructional design.

Because the process draws much of its strength from participative brainstorming, the designer must respond to opinions and suggestions with sensitivity. Timing is part of this, as is deciding when to respond and when to simply observe the

process quietly. The task requires interpersonal effectiveness just as much as it requires knowledge of learning and instruction. This is the real world for instructional designers.

It is not enough for today's designers to produce optimal learning experiences, as difficult as that is; they must also contend with and manage the varying expectations, preferences, and constraints imposed by project sponsors. They must design interactions that can be developed using tools known by and available to developers (regardless of their

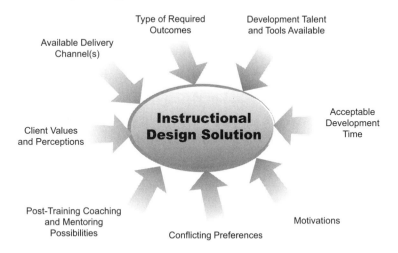

A sampling of factors impinging on instructional design

suitability) and within time constraints. The possibility of training supervisors or on-the-job mentors to new learners may be limited or impossible. And the challenges go on.

Challenges of teams

Brainstorming sessions sometimes conjure up design ideas that are plagued with problems. The problems may lie in unrealistic development expense, ineffectual design, overgeneralization of research findings, or elsewhere. If you, as the designer, keep quiet, the group may continue to list other, more realistic ideas and never come back to problematic ones, in which case, keeping quiet was probably smart, although the group missed the benefit of learning from you. Sometimes the group will become increasingly enamored with a clearly bad design, and they need to be pushed off it as quickly as possible. It's a judgment call.

To fulfill your role as instructional designer, it's important to know what works and what doesn't—or, because design choices are seldom black and white, what is more or less likely to work. It's important to assess situations quickly and explain your opinion in simple terms, with examples whenever possible. You need to be open to new ideas and proposals too, knowing that there's no one perfect design.

Even if there were a perfect design, it might be unrealistically hard to get the group's support for it. So you will be searching for a design that both succeeds in winning critical support and succeeds with learners.

Your first choice is not an option

In the first book of the series, we reviewed being realistic about the challenges, needs, and opportunities most e-learning projects have, especially when the project is responsible to a committee. We stressed the need, for example, to identify the key decision maker and secure his or her involvement at critical times, even though the individual may wish to remain unidentified or uninvolved. His or her opinions will surface at some point, and although praise is welcome any time, divergent thought delivered late in the process can be devastating.

By waiting until late in the process, decision makers have the opportunity to say, *That's not at all what I wanted,* when, indeed, they had no idea of what they wanted before you produced a solution.

One's first choice is rarely an option. To be helpful under the broad range of typical and sometimes nearly overwhelming challenges that designers face, we draw on lessons learned from designers who are successful in both creating powerful learning experiences and reshaping designs to comply with organizational constraints and idiosyncrasies. These lessons bridge gaps between well-established principles of learning design and provide suggestions of what to do when one's first choice is not an option.

And as if that weren't enough

The bubble has burst. We've been laboring under the assumption that if we could just make learning events more effective, we would deliver the performance needed. As we'll find out in Chapter 7, research tells us not to expect behavioral change to come simply from instruction. We shouldn't, in fact, even expect much learning to occur unless we look beyond the bounds of typical instructional events to prepare learners for the process and to support them in the process of transferring learning into successful performance.

As frustrating as it may feel to add yet more challenges and tasks to the process of creating successful e-learning, it's quite exciting to sense a breakthrough of understanding why so many learning interventions, offered through e-learning and other formats, have failed to produce superior performance. I now see the breakthrough coming from the merger of successful learning paradigms with techniques that have proven successful in helping individuals change (psychotherapy of change) and with organizational change (change management).

The next chapter sets forth the framework, which is a combination of all that we've covered so far with exciting insights from the science of behavioral change and concepts of change management. This merger of principles and techniques provides a new view—perhaps a revitalizing view—of how we can help people and organizations realize their performance potential. Stay with me. This is going to be fun!

7 | Designing Outside the Box

Remember Bill Hamm (from scenario 1)? Bill brought successes to Hoboken Automotive Devices not because he held with tradition but because he focused on needed outcomes—intensely focused on needed outcomes. Every decision he made and direction he gave was based on its value for achieving the targeted performance.

He was more concerned, for example, with recognizing learners as people than with the "proper" sequencing of content. Even if content were perfectly sequenced (whatever that is), even sequenced perfectly and specifically for a specific learner, that learner might still opt to browse about—picking things up in something of a haphazard sequence or purposely creating puzzles to solve and getting involved. (Remember, we don't always want things to be as easy as possible.)

Bill was also more concerned with making sure learners would be prepared to learn, focused on the outcomes, and committed to improvement before they began learning how to improve. And he took proactive steps to provide a supportive environment among coworkers, supervisors, and management, even in different divisions of the company.

Buried in a box

We often think too narrowly of our role as instructional designers, confining our work to the definition of objectives, organizing content, selecting media, defining learning events, and developing performance measures (tests). Not that this isn't more than enough to do, but our role as instructional designers isn't simply to apply design principles and hope for the best; it's to enable people to perform at higher levels of competency. And that takes what it takes.

If our learners fail in performance, we have failed them, even if they scored flawlessly on our posttest. Excuses that learners would do fine if only they completed all of our e-learning modules, if only they did their homework, if only they'd practice more, if only they'd take a chance and apply the new things we've taught

Яapid readeR

- External factors preceding, concurrent with, and following instruction affect learning and subsequent performance.

- Instructional design needs to address factors outside "the box" of instructional events.

- The psychology of behavioral change suggests ways to improve the impact of instructional interventions.

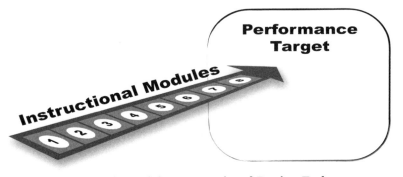

Boxed View of the Instructional Design Task

them, are just that: excuses. We've failed to reach the goal even if any of these things "explain" the failure. Designing inside the "boxes" of an e-learning application, an instructor-led course, or even a blended learning solution, is a traditional but narrow view of the design responsibility. Inside these boxes, designers often give little attention

to the practicality of learners actually performing on the job what they are teaching, the level of practice that is necessary to sustain proficiency when performance opportunities might not occur for some time, and the fact that coworkers might misunderstand or even disapprove of the new practices being taught.

No, they create a string of learning modules, each dependent on the preceding one, each presenting more difficult concepts and tasks to perform, each designed to raise performance to a higher level. There's an assumption that the learner is totally inside each box with the designer—committed to and focused on each module, approaching it with energy and enthusiasm.

We designers need to get out more—out of our boxes, that is. There are many variables not typically seen as within the purview of instructional design that can sabotage instructional efforts or enrich them. Success requires designers to think expansively about the real lives and influences on learners—what they care about, what they are trying to do, how they might perceive the learning intervention—and design both inside and outside the confines of the typical learning product.

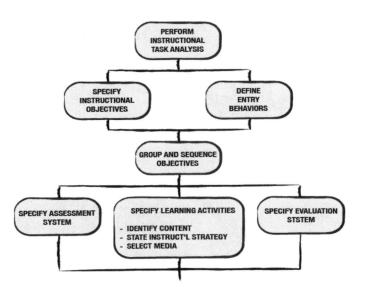

Some of the Traditional Design Boxes

Failure to do so may result in great ideas being buried quite prematurely in the very large box of quickly retired learning programs.

Broader perspectives

Learning and performance occur inside a large and complex landscape of overlapping contexts. Organizational, family, and personal contexts are a few of the obvious larger contexts, and these are themselves comprised of many subcontexts, ultimately bombarding people with a cacophony of directives.

For example, while we might like to think our travel agent trainee has little excuse not to learn and apply best practices, life is rarely that simple. *I really should get back to my client with available flight information before the end of the lunch hour, but I have such a headache. If I don't take a break and eat now, I won't be back at my desk when my boss returns from her lunch. My client might be unhappy, but I'd rather have that than an unhappy boss. Of course, if my boss finds out my client is unhappy, I'll have both. OK, I'm going for a walk.*

Each context has numerous operational elements that strongly affect what people do, what they perceive, and what happens in their

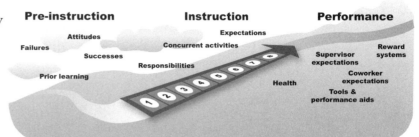

Putting the Design Challenge in Context

minds as they work through a learning program. As a learning program begins, learners set out with their preconceptions of what they think they're going to learn, what they're supposed to learn, why someone else thinks they should learn it, how easy or difficult it will be, and so on. They recall previous successes and failures in learning related content, *I'm just not good at anything to do with math,* in attempts to perform similar tasks, *I get so nervous whenever I work with financials,* and in learning other subjects through similar methods, *Remember that "really complicated" e-learning we had to take on expense reports?* Eagerness to use e-learning and expectations about using it are influenced by prior experiences with it and what one has heard about it.

As learners use e-learning, they are also influenced by other things going on in their lives. If learning is occurring in a work or school environment, for example, learners will be influenced by assignments they may have, responsibilities they must attend to, and expectations others have of them, *Did you get the munchies for the party tonight?* If you're a learner and others perceive you to be strong in the content area, you may be afraid of exposing any weaknesses through errors or poor scores. If others expect you to do poorly, you may struggle fretfully to gather confidence.

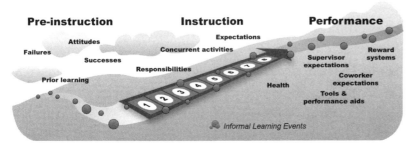

Informal Learning

A very large contextual influence often comes from informal learning events. Informal learning is learning that occurs by casual observation, discussion around the water cooler, reading a pamphlet in the waiting room, e-mailing a friend, or reading a blog.

While formal learning is comprised of prestructured events,

thoughtfully constructed for accuracy and completeness and often imposed on learners, ready or not, informal learning is more serendipitous. Learners approach, select, and personalize the experiences they have, sometimes initiated quite intentionally, but often occurring in an *ad hoc* manner. "It's all a matter of learning, but it's not the sort of learning that is the province of training departments, workshops, and classrooms" (Cross, 2003).

Indeed, researchers suggest that 75-90 percent of learning comes not from formally structured learning events, but from informal learning experiences (Cross, 2007). Informal can be sufficient on its own or assist more formal efforts, but just as it can be a boon, it can also confuse learn-

Resources

Cross, J. (2003). Informal learning – the other 80%. Internet Time Group. Retrieved on Oct. 20, 2006 from http://www. internettime.com/Learning/ The%20Other%2080%25.htm.

Cross, J. (2007). *Informal Learning: Rediscovering the Natural Pathways that Inspire Innovation and Performance*. San Francisco: Pfeiffer.

ers, promulgate misinformation, and decrease the efficiency of an organization. As such a major contextual factor, despite how often it's ignored in the creation of instructional programs, we add informal learning to our visualization of the learning landscape and later address ways designers can work with informal learning as a tool to achieve desired behavioral outcomes.

Working the larger contexts

I've written and spoken extensively about the necessity of learner motivation and ways to motivate learners through e-learning design. In *Michael Allen's Guide to e-Learning* (Allen, 2003), I identified seven particularly powerful ways to make learning experiences engaging and motivational. We'll review the Seven Magic Keys to motivating e-learners later when we address designing interactivity, because these techniques are both amazingly effective and yet frequently omitted. But as frequently as learner motivation is left unaddressed by designers, other contextual issues that have a profound impact on learning and behavior are even more commonly overlooked.

As the figure on the previous page conveys, the three sequential and overlapping contexts surround the path to desired performance, influencing learning and resultant behavioral change along the way. These contextual phases are: *Pre-instruction,* which include attitudes, motivations, and skills developed before formalized training begins on the current topic; *Instruction,* which includes all the behavior and attention-influencing factors concurrent with training; and *Performance,* which includes all behavioral influences extant after training has concluded and new ones emanating when improved performance is expected.

Pre-instruction phase

Learners are anything but a blank slate. They may not know much about the content and skills to be learned, but learners approach learning with various levels of confidence, expectations, readiness, habits, and preferences. They have both a general disposition in each of these factors as well as more specific dispositions with respect to the content or (whatever they know of it) and what they may know of e-learning and other instructional techniques involved (or expected to be involved).

The period preceding instruction is an important time for (re)setting expectations, energizing learners, and preparing them to learn. Some relevant learning may be happening through informal means, such as peer mentoring or self-improvement efforts, as learners prepare for scheduled learning events. While some of this learning can be helpful, with no support or organization, it will be serendipitous, incomplete, and possibly misguided.

Instruction phase

The Instruction phase is where the organized intervention of teaching takes place with the intent of moving the learner from current levels of capability and performance to more effective and valuable levels.

Although Instruction is the phase in the formalized learning process on which designers traditionally focus their efforts—all of their efforts—here too, there is a larger domain of learning opportunities. Properly harnessed, some contextual influences can become effective learning aids and some impeding influences can be mitigated. It's important for designers to recognize and give attention to the surrounding environment, taking advantage, for example, of the support and energy concurrent learners can provide to each other.

Performance phase

Designers often act like parental turtles, walking off the job when their eggs hatch and leaving their young to fend for themselves. But embryonic skills face a high fatality rate when support terminates at the end of formalized instruction.

Just as only one in one hundred hatchling turtles survive to juvenility, designers leave much to chance if they view what happens to learners after instruction as something that is completely outside their realm of influence. Throughout all three phases, which repeat over and over in our lives, many surrounding factors work against change, even beneficial changes. Designers need to recognize and mitigate adverse factors where possible and devise safeguards and support mechanisms so that nascent abilities can be fully developed along with performance confidence.

Accumulating influences

Shaping and reinforcing behavior patterns, sometimes over the course of many years, the collection of memories and emotions that influence us presents real obstacles to behavioral change. We work hard to achieve comfort and find ways to assimilate new experiences and values with minimal upheaval. Rather than replacing them with memories of new occurrences in subsequent contexts, experiences and their effects accumulate and intermix with those of newer contexts. And because of the cumulative, interactive, complex, and persistent nature of all these experiences, perceptions, and values, they are formidable determinants of behavior, indeed. We shouldn't expect change to be easy.

And yet, it's not always a tough situation. Learners are sometimes positively poised for change. Their prior experiences are positively aligned and nourish both the learning and behavioral changes we are trying to achieve. Other times there are few active influences; they neither support undesired behaviors nor inhibit desired ones. Here too, it's important for designers not to overlook the positive influences that can be commandeered.

Learning and contextual factors are important. Working with contextual factors may achieve a major portion, if not all, of the desired outcomes an instructional program is being created to achieve. For example, helping capable learners set appropriate goals, commit to a program of change, and make contact with other learners targeting the same goals may be enough. Arranging this can require some actions that are very much outside the normal duties of instructional designers, but are nevertheless necessary if any performance intervention can have hope of success.

The design challenge

Behavioral patterns are difficult to change. They tend to persist even when a simple variation might be both pleasant and beneficial to the performer and everyone surrounding him or her. There are many reasons we form consistent behavioral patterns, even when there may be better options. A few are:

➤ Familiar responses take less energy than crafting and executing new ones. Our brains are wired to conserve energy.

➤ We can perform practiced behaviors faster than new ones.

65

Sticking with old behaviors saves time.

➤ Behaviors that were successful in the past are likely to be successful again. Repeating them incurs less risk of failure than trying something else.

➤ Our behaviors reconfirm who we are, both for ourselves and for others. This consistency is comforting and continually reinforced if even by just the slightest nonverbal recognition by others.

Many, many factors inhibit change, and instructional efforts can directly address very few of them, indeed. When we evaluate instruction based on the extent to which it leads to improved behavior, we realize we're asking it to do something that's often tremendously difficult, especially when that improvement is in real-world performance, as opposed to just correct answers—on a test.

The psychology of behavioral change

In broadening the scope of instructional design, beyond the confines of "simply" designing learning activities, and to engage the full challenge of enabling superior performance, it's prudent to ask what other efforts

to modify human behavior yield guidance. Are there techniques employed by psychologists, for example, which are effective in helping people change their behaviors? If so, do these techniques identify possible ways to increase the effectiveness of instructional programs?

James Prochaska and colleagues, John Norcross and Carlo DiClemente (1994), have identified stages of behavioral change in a model that deserves consideration by instructional designers. Although this work has focused primarily on weight reduction, drug addiction, anger management, smoking cessation, and lifestyle behaviors, its effectiveness for behavioral change has been verified by considerable research. The clarity of its structure yields relatively clear implications for instructional design, especially when taking the broader view of instructional design, which expands to preinstruction, concurrent instructional

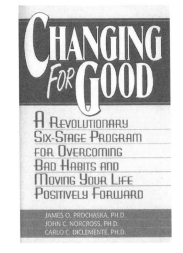

Resource

Prochaska, J.O., Norcross, J.C. and DiClemente, C. C. (1994). *Changing for Good: A Revolutionary Six-Stage Program for Overcoming Bad Habits and Moving Your Life Positively Forward.* NY: Quill.

contexts, and transfer of training to performance. If this model can be effective for combating entrenched, even physically addictive behaviors, it would seem that it might be even more effective when the change-opposing forces were milder.

Stages of Change model

The *Stages of Change* model postulates that there is a course of successful change comprised of six well-defined stages (p. 39):

1. Precontemplation
2. Contemplation
3. Preparation
4. Action
5. Maintenance
6. Termination

Each stage serves as a prerequisite to the following stage, with almost all changes beginning in the Precontemplation stage. Most interestingly, the model claims that stages cannot be skipped for successful, sustained change. Each stage requires different activities and achievements before one can successfully engage the next stage.

Precontemplation stage

In the *Precontemplation stage,* people don't see problems arising from their own behavior. They don't want to change and don't see the need to. If they recognize a problem, they see it as caused by others or by external factors outside their control. People in this stage can be pressured into changing exhibited behaviors, but will quickly revert to previous patterns as soon as the pressure abates. As changers progress through this stage, they begin to focus more on the reasons to change and less on the sacrifices change would require.

Contemplation stage

At the start of the *Contemplation stage*, people focus on their problems, dwell in its causes, but also ponder solutions. These ruminations don't necessarily indicate readiness to commit to a solution or, in fact, any action at all, just the consideration. Contemplation is as far as many people get for weight loss, fitness, or smoking cessation.

Contemplators transition through this stage by focusing more on the solution than the problem and to imagining how much better things will be when their problem is solved. Although anxious, they become excited and hopeful about making a change.

Preparation stage

In the *Preparation stage*, people begin making concrete plans for change. This is a point where a realistic appraisal leads to identifying strategies not only for moving forward, but also for handling setbacks when they occur. This is also a point of making a commitment. It helps to make that commitment not only to yourself but also more publicly to others.

Cutting preparation too short often results in setbacks, but taking too long risks regressing back to contemplation.

Action stage

In the *Action stage*, people make changes to their behavior. Although it would seem that the purpose of the entire change process is to achieve appropriate actions, the Prochaska team warns that a few appropriate actions don't equate to change. Aligning emotions and self-image with successful performance is just as critical as sharpening skills to detect situations in which different behaviors are effective. This stage begins the practice that is critical to substituting good habits for bad.

Maintenance Stage

In the *Maintenance stage*, one has to maintain vigilance to keep from slipping back into poor habits. If reinforcements for poor behaviors have not been removed from the environment, this vigilance requires constant energy and may need to persist for a long time. One slip can begin a pattern of a few slips here and there. A complete relapse is then imminent.

Termination stage

Termination of undesired behavior and substitution of desirable behaviors is the ultimate goal of change. In the Termination stage, the temptation to revert to previous behaviors no longer represents any threat. Even without exerting the effort required for vigilance in the Maintenance stage, those who have terminated undesirable habits have no likelihood of falling back to undesirable behavioral patterns.

A key to successful change is in knowing what stage you are in for the problem at hand. Our research has consistently shown that people who try to accomplish changes they are not ready for set themselves up for failure. Similarly, if you spend too much time working on tasks you have already mastered—such as understanding your problem—you may delay acting upon it indefinitely. Matching your challenges to your stage of change will help maximize your problem-solving efforts (p. 39).

Parallels to learning for performance improvement

The work of Prochaska, Norcross, and DiClimente has focused on overcoming bad habits, even addictions, and replacing them with more desirable behaviors. Changing these problematic behaviors is difficult, whether people undertake efforts to change on their own or with professional help. Such changes could be considered to fall at the extreme end of a continuum of difficulty, whereas the typical changes sought from learning and training programs might cover the area from easy to moderately difficult. In addition, some behavioral change objectives might not involve supplanting conflicting behaviors but simply developing new skills, such as learning to count or how to shut down a computer.

The process of teaching new behaviors for performance at work or in one's intellectual life is arguably quite different from the process of eliminating personally destructive habits or replacing bad habits with good ones, but the parallels between the processes are striking nevertheless.

First, just as we cannot change the voluntary behavior of others, neither can we learn for people. Setting traumatic events aside, to change their habits, people must come to want change, commit to change, and work to make it happen. To learn, people must want to learn, commit to learning, and work to make it happen. Very similar.

Second, new behaviors are often difficult to instill. The failure of many instructional programs to generate measurably improved performance, despite earnest efforts by organizations, attests to the fact that there are powerful forces resisting change, whether lifestyle or performance related. While some behaviors can be changed as simply as issuing a directive or erecting a barrier—*The rear door is no longer to be used except in an emergency. It now sounds an alarm when opened.*—many behaviors are much more complex and extremely resistant to change.

> **Think**
>
> How is the process of changing lifestyle behaviors different from changing other behaviors?

69

Third, it's easy to blame poor performance on external factors, just as it's easy to abrogate responsibility for bad habits and project blame on others or uncontrollable situations. *I know I should develop a sales strategy for each account, but it takes so long to enter the data in our system.* This doesn't sound much different from: *I don't have much time to eat lunch, and the fast foods they serve are unavoidably high in fats and calories.* Taking responsibility for your behavior is critical to changing it in both cases.

Fourth, lacking confidence in themselves, many people don't take the risk of applying newly learned skills. If they aren't applied reasonably soon after acquisition, of course, new skills fade rapidly. This failure to achieve behavioral improvement correlates with the pattern of those having poor self-esteem, who blame themselves for characteristic weaknesses and make only half-hearted attempts to terminate bad habits. When they fail once or twice, they quickly give up, sometimes even taking comfort from accurately predicting that they wouldn't be able to do it. *See, I knew I couldn't do it.*

Fifth, denying or minimizing the effects of one's flawed behavior provides an excuse for not acquiring new skills and changing behavior. *I might not be the most knowledgeable or meticulous painter on our team, but if people didn't complain about my goofs, they'd complain about the quality of the paint, the color, the cost of the job, or something else.* Not much different from: *Sure, I smoke a little. But one day, fat is bad for you; the next day, high fat diets are all the rage. Soon, they'll find smoking has benefits. Besides, George Burns smoked as many as 10 cigars a day until his death, and he lived 100 years!*

If the case weren't strong enough already, two additional parallels are very interesting:

1. Much contemporary instructional design is based on behaviorism or retains at least a strong flavor of it. *Simply get people to respond as we wish, provide knowledge of results as a reward, and practice until correct responses meet criteria.* Unfortunately, this approach, while quite effective with mice and pigeons to "teach" them relatively simple behaviors, has not worked as well with humans. It does not embrace the complex-

ity of human thinking, emotions, motivation, and the powerful effects of the environment in which people behave.

Similarly, in psychotherapy for behavioral problems, ...

> The action paradigm has dominated behavioral change programs for the past three or four decades. Following this model, clients are enrolled in relatively brief programs designed to conquer smoking, weight, alcohol, or other problems; within weeks they are expected to take action and adopt healthier lifestyles. If they fail to take or maintain action, the clients themselves are blamed for a lack of willpower or motivation (Prochaska, et al., p. 15).

2. Instructional designers have long been looking for more effective design models that, because they are based on a robust mapping of human behavior, are reliable and well structured. Similarly, Prochaska, et al. wanted to know if there were basic principles that reveal the structure of change.

> In more than fifty studies of thousands of individuals attempting to overcome behavioral problems, Prochaska, et al. discovered that the sequence of successful change required preparation in advance of simple action. Mental and emo-

tional preparation, for example, is critical for modified actions to take root and last (p. 14).

This observation couldn't be more similar to the instructional design advice given to us by many researchers and instructional design experts. Learners need to be ready, motivated, and focused.

There may be additional parallels between the processes of changing personal habits and learning for performance change, but we have enough impressive similarities identified to explore how the understanding of behavioral change revealed by the Prochaska Stages of Change model can lead to more effective e-learning design.

Aligning stages of change

It would be interesting if the Stages of Change aligned directly with learning contexts, but some stages

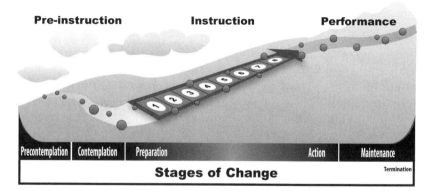

71

would seem to overlap learning phases. The appropriate alignment is, arguably, as shown in the figure on the previous page.

The Precontemplation and Contemplation stages define processes that would be most helpful if they were completed before undertaking the instruction to learn how to behave more effectively. If learners have no interest or intent to learn or perform new skills (the question of *whether* to do anything at all), instructional events will have little effect (the question of *how* to do things). We show these two stages occurring in the Pre-instruction phase.

A commitment to improve behavior can greatly increase the effectiveness of an instructional program and the likelihood of successful change. In the Stages of Change model, commitment is a process that occurs in the Preparation stage. We therefore show Preparation beginning before the onset of instruction. Because instruction can help learners further their commitment to change and make more effective plans for acquiring and implementing new behaviors, we show Preparation continuing well into the Instruction

phase and blending into the Action stage.

We show the Preparation and Action stages blending together because it is effective to make plans, take corresponding action, and then make additional plans for the next actions. In other words, learners may find it strategic and beneficial to bounce back and forth a bit between these two stages. Note that we also show the Action stage overlapping the Instruction phase because learners can begin to take action, even if just in simulation, with the guidance of e-learning.

The new behaviors targeted by both the change and training processes are applied and practiced subsequent to the Instructional phase and hopefully continue long after. We therefore place much of the Action stage in the Performance phase along with the Maintenance and Termination stages. Maintenance is especially important for tasks that are not performed often and for situations in which there are temptations to cut corners, revert to prior habits, or otherwise perform less than optimally.

Termination is perhaps a concept that applies less well than others to training and education. It does, of course, represent the targeted performance context, however idealistic, in which there is no longer any likelihood that the learner's performance will lapse. Here, we have terminated either ineffective behaviors or the habit of taking no action when action is called for and see targeted behaviors occurring instead.

Implications for instructional design

Stages of Change research focuses on the complexities of human behavior that make change difficult. It focuses on a wide range of human behaviors, from kicking destructive and potential fatal habits to making changes for improved family or work life. Why do people do what is harmful to themselves? Why do they not change when the harm they are causing is so extreme as to be fatal in the long run? Why do workaholics sacrifice time with their children that can never be replaced? Why do people eat when they aren't hungry, stay up too late, or fail to listen attentively? Although many of the behavioral challenges the Prochaska team faces are much more recalcitrant than those faced by trainers and educators, the failure of so many instructional programs to yield

performance improvements suggests that we have been underestimating the challenges even simple change presents.

Prochaska, et al. provide not only an understanding of the stages through which changers progress to reach their goals, but also, as we shall see in the next chapter, a compilation and synthesis of techniques used to help people along the way. Quite specific techniques, such as raising consciousness, social liberation, and emotional arousal, are found to be effective at identified points of the process. These various techniques can be applied in part or whole through the interactive capabilities of e-learning, and comprise what might come to be recognized as "the missing" e-learning techniques—what e-learning has needed to achieve its full potential.

The focus of instructional programs is to help people acquire the knowledge and skills necessary to behave more effectively. The most powerful programs are complementary to helping people overcome their resistance to change because they focus not simply on teaching recognition and recall skills, but also on problem-solving skills, recognizing situations for which certain behaviors are appropriate and for which others are not, adapting solutions as specific conditions warrant, and evaluating the success of applied solutions. When targeted behaviors are complex, effective instructional techniques become crucial for the success of any change initiative. Clearly, if people don't know how to behave more effectively, they won't, no matter how determined they become to do so.

Pre-instruction

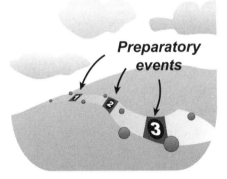

Preparatory events

Stages of Change-based help programs teach people the *reasons* change is important, *methods* of preparing for change, and *actions* to take to overcome problematic behavior. This approach correlates well with many instructional design theories. And the concurrence continues as both processes also need to be sure learner/changers *are motivated* to learn, *are committed* to making changes, *make effective plans* to learn and change, *put appropriate actions in place* to transfer learning to real situations, and *practice sufficiently* to make new behaviors resilient.

Expanding the purview of instructional design

Aligning the process of change with the process of instruction suggests the need for instructional design to address a broader range of needs. Since cognitive and affective preparation is essential for effective learning to occur, and since performance must be guided and nurtured for an extended period after new skills are learned, instructional design attention should extend into both the Pre-instruction and Performance contexts. Addressing these additional needs appears fundamental to achieving difficult behavioral changes and may also provide the key as to why otherwise well-designed instructional events fail to have the intended impact.

To reflect these insights, we can begin to modify the diagram of the instruction/learning/change process by adding events as shown here. What's changed? Interactive activities are introduced before the Instruction phase, but instead of focusing primarily on developing targeted skills, these activities provide information and learning experiences designed to help learners contemplate and prepare for making behavioral changes.

Providing preparatory events to precede formal learning events isn't really anything new, but the nature of them as suggested by Stages of Change is. For example, instead of simply giving learners preparatory reading to help reduce variance in readiness to learn, suggested preparatory events use such techniques as raising consciousness, social liberation, and self-reevaluation to help learners focus on behavioral changes and commit to the process of achieving them.

This approach points to ways we can release instruction from the controlled and constrained context that many adult learners abhor and fit it into the larger stream-of-life context. That's not to say that this broader perspective and framework are more fitting for training than education. Nor is it to say that this framework wouldn't be far more effective for academic application than the traditional methods of educational institutions. It appears, rather, that this framework recognizes the true needs humans have when more effective behaviors are targeted and begins to give us a blueprint for designing more effective and interesting learning aids.

This view also recognizes that new skills are often difficult for learners to apply outside the support and cues provided in learning environments where all the familiar cues and support systems for prior behaviors exist, prompting learners to behave as they did before they learned new ways. If opportunities to rehearse new skills don't come immediately or often, newly learned behaviors stand a strong risk of being forgotten.

Effective design work combats these barriers to change by offering learners assistance with the transference of training to application in the real world. For example, learners often find reminders, checklists, recurrent training, and feedback systems of great help. Supervisor training may make the difference between success and failure because their ability to coach learners in application of their new skills is often pivotal.

By the way, organizations that try to make changes without recognizing the influence of supervisors are

Performance

Practice and transfer aids

often puzzled about why behavioral changes are so difficult to effect. Supervisors are powerful influencers. They can provide essential feedback and reinforcement, making change programs highly successful. Conversely, they may find changes in behavior patterns unsettling and annoying. Communicating their stance to subordinates, even subtly, can squash their attempts to apply newly learned behaviors.

Spaced learning events

Spacing is defined as the distribution of learning events over time. For example, instead of learning how to write useful objective statements in one full-day class, an e-learning application might introduce the key concepts and provide practice for an hour or less. The next day, learners would review the concepts and do more exercises. Perhaps a week later, learners would do still more exercises, and then maybe a month later, the final set.

With spaced learning, learning time is more efficient (less total time is required) and learning is retained for a longer period of time. Ideally, the spaces between practice sessions increase to equal the time between actual events in which learners will perform the learned tasks (Thalheimer, 2006). That is, if learners evaluate job applications only twice each month, practice sessions will grow to be spaced about two weeks apart.

"The spacing effect is one of the oldest and best documented phenomena in the history of learning and memory research" (Bahrick and Hall, 2005, p. 566). Spacing saves learning time and produces superior results, although it's a technique that I find seldom used in e-learning—an observation that seems odd given that e-learning can provide individualized spacing that might be difficult to schedule for a group. Repeatedly requiring learners to assess a situation, recall information, and apply a skill is better than no

Resources

⌨ Thalheimer, W. (2006). Spacing learning events over time: What the research says. Retrieved October 15, 2006, from http://www.work-learning. com/catalog/

📖 Bahrick, H.P. and Hall, L.K. (2005). The importance of retrieval failures to long-term retention: A metacognitive explanation of the spacing effect. *Journal of Memory and Language*, 52(4) 566-577.

repetition—and we also see far too little practice in most designs, but spacing the repetitions is better yet, and increasingly spaced repetitions are best.

We'll review spacing again as we talk more specifically about designing learning events, but for now, we'll adjust the visual of the learning process to show spaced learning events.

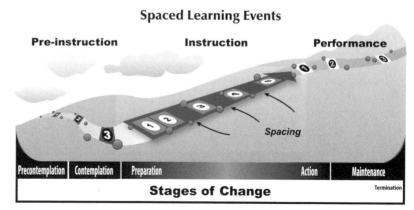

Using the savings

Adding pre-instruction and performance modules to e-learning applications may be essential to achieving great success (and a great ROI), but there are obviously associated costs. These costs are not always significant, but are almost always worth the expense. A highly motivated, ready-to-learn learner is much more likely to actually learn and need less support. Added to the fact that, the impact of spaced learning is much higher than the impact of massed learning events, it may be possible to develop much more effective e-learning at the same cost as ineffective learning. Fewer "traditional" learning events can be developed while a few additional interactive events are spaced through the Pre-instruction and Performance phases.

The optimal target may be the one represented in the figure above in which learning activities help prepare learners for change, help prepare learners for learning, help learners develop needed knowledge and skills, help learners apply their new abilities in actual situations, and then help learners maintain and refine their skills in practice.

Informal learning

Finally, but definitely not to be forgotten, we turn to the effects of and opportunities with informal learning. We learn things every day, regardless of whether we attend classes or use e-learning. *Informal learning* is defined simply as learning that occurs outside of events specifically designed to result in learning outcomes. Examples of informal learning include serendipitous

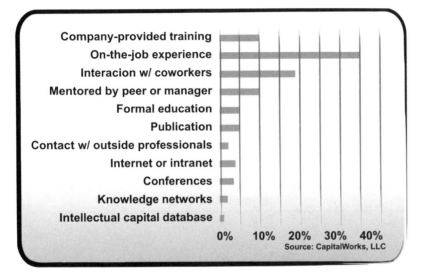

Company-provided training
On-the-job experience
Interacion w/ coworkers
Mentored by peer or manager
Formal education
Publication
Contact w/ outside professionals
Internet or intranet
Conferences
Knowledge networks
Intellectual capital database

0%   10%   20%   30%   40%
Source: CapitalWorks, LLC

How Workers Report Learning To Do Their Jobs

learning through lunch discussions, browsing through a catalog, and assembling a kit airplane.

Through informal learning, learners make discoveries from real-life experiences and from socially based interactions with coworkers, mentors, and coaches. These interactions provide a basis for modeling behaviors, gaining on-the-job proficiencies, and adapting to continuously changing work environments. Nuances not easily captured in instructional design efforts nor conveyed well to learners in more formal contexts are easily, and often enthusiastically, conveyed informally. *We're supposed to complete account strategy reports on every identified account, but Marilyn is much happier with just*

a few detailed strategies than a boatload of drivel. Not only is informal learning more personal, contextually relevant, memorable, and applicable in business settings, it also leverages learners' versatility in adapting to future conditions and establishing greater connectivity within these settings (Cross, 2003).

Kelley (2001) provides an interesting breakdown of how we learn in the work environment.

On-the-job experience was reported to be the largest single source of learning in the workplace, by far. This category can include a host of things, of course, even such everyday experiences as trial-and-error attempts to fix a copy machine. The message is clear, and really not surprising as we think about how one becomes proficient in any job, that most of what we learn and apply comes through personally directed, informal learning experiences.

Just as with learner motivation, where instructional interventions need not be helpless victims of low motivation levels, instructional designers can increase the quality and impact of informal learning. We will review methods of doing this in later chapters.

Blended learning

We conclude this chapter, which explores the need for instructional designers to work outside the confines of isolated instructional events, with a few thoughts on blended learning.

I have been resistant to what appeared at first blush to be yet another fad in the never-ending search for a simple, quick, and easy way to create high-impact, learning events. *Blended learning* appeared to be a regression to instructor-led learning as a fix for ineffective e-learning. Indeed, it is often just that. When e-learning fails to motivate learners, adapt to their individual needs, and provide authentic learning experiences that transfer to the real world, some fix is certainly needed. Since so much e-learning has these weaknesses, complementing it with other experiences that might do better in these regards can help.

But face-to-face, group, synchronous distance, and other forms of instructional-led learning are not reliably better with respect to motivating learners, adapting to the individual needs, and providing authentic learning experiences. It is, in fact, these typical weaknesses of

instruction that motivated pioneers in e-learning to seek alternatives (Allen, in press). And in all cases, it's not the channel of delivery that determines outcomes; it's the quality of the instructional design.

Resources

📖 Allen, M.W. (Ed.). (in press). *Michael Allen's e-Learning Annual.* San Francisco: Pfeiffer.

📖 Kelley, J.D. (2001). *Developing and Applying a Learning Effectiveness Index: Preliminary Findings Report.* Williamstown, MA: CapitalWorks, LLC.

However, by looking at the multifarious factors that determine behavior and resist its change, it now becomes clear that some form of blending is essential in many situations. The blending concept that is essential, however, may be less focused on delivery channels and more a blending of purposes. We need activities to enhance the learners' emotional readiness to learn, create a groundswell of social support for behavioral change, provide incentives for performance improvement, provide feedback to guide changers, and train supervisors for mentoring. This is blended learning that makes sense and will undoubtedly result in success.

Summary

As complex as instructional design is, typical processes tend to oversimplify the view of what causes people to behave as they do, whether it's in learning experiences, on the job, or elsewhere. As a result, popular techniques often focus on design details while missing the big picture and not targeting the most significant issues.

It's time to forget some of the detail and connect with the major issues. People are busy, familiar with current routine, and frightened of change. People don't improve their performance just because someone tells them to, because they know how, or because they will be rewarded for it (behaviorism). In fact, if they feel manipulated, their natural response is to fight back.

There are three contexts of concern: the Pre-instruction phase, the Instruction phase, and the Performance phase. While designers have naturally focused on teaching knowledge and skills in the instruction phase, behaviors seldom change if learners are not committed to change and work through a process of change. The Prochaska, et al. Stages of Change model identifies a well-validated process of change that we have aligned with the phases of learning. This alignment calls out ways to help learners focus on and achieve the changes that learning interventions are designed to accomplish. It expands the province of and challenge to instructional design. It pushes us out of the box.

Part Three
Designing Successful e-Learning

Dickie was a hard worker. As a laborer for a landscape contractor we had hired, he was laying concrete block for steps and planters behind our house. He showed up early every day and worked hard. He spoke Jamaican Creole or patois and a little English, although he understood it well.

Unfortunately, Dickie wasn't very meticulous about his work. Instead of measuring carefully and setting up guidelines, he worked by eye. After he had worked several days, we noticed he was veering off course considerably. Block rows had rises and dips that became more severe with each added course. This clearly wasn't satisfactory, and we alerted the contractor. The contractor agreed that the work wasn't acceptable and hired a construction company to come in and fix the problem.

Dickie, however, wasn't about to be dismissed. He had an agreement that paid him when the walls, steps, and planters were finished. He intended to keep working and collect upon setting the last block. He understood that the work wasn't satisfactory, but that didn't dissuade him in the slightest.

Picture this, if you will. It really happened. The construction company realized that the blocks had to be removed and re-laid from the bottom up. They came in to remove them, but Dickie refused to leave the job or back up for correction. So, as Dickie scooped up concrete, spread it on rows of blocks, and built up walls, the crew followed along behind Dickie removing blocks, tearing down walls, and cleaning up blocks to be reset.

Sometimes we have to step back to take a broader perspective.

If we were more realistic about the determinants of behavior, would we design e-learning differently?

The timeline of learning and applying new skills has three phases: the Pre-Instruction phase, Instruction phase, and Performance phase. While instructional programs have typically jumped immediately into learning events, it is often well worth the time and effort to prepare learners first. With effective preparation for learning and a firm commitment to applying new skills, instructional programs can have far greater impact.

In the Instruction phase, e-learning programs need to provide meaningful, memorable, and motivational experiences if we expect learners to do anything beyond achieving good posttest scores. Chapters 9 through 12 traverse important concepts that can help instructional designers design high-impact learning experiences.

Finally, in Chapter 13, we look at techniques to help learners gain confidence and perfect their skills as they apply them and gradually wean themselves from the support of the learning environment.

Chapter 8—Designing Pre-Instructional Events

Chapter 8 looks at the influences that may affect a learner's inter-est and ability to learn. Without addressing some readiness factors, instructional interventions may be useless. On the other hand, with proper orientation and learner disposition, programs that might be moderately successful can become much more successful. Preparation techniques can be delivered through e-learning, through face-to-face programs, or through blended delivery.

Major topics include:

Potent preludes
Achieving impact
Change is difficult
    Facilitating change
    Raising learner consciousness
    The change campaign
    Facilitating social liberation
    Self-evaluation through e-learning
    Engaging emotions
    Fostering commitment
    Maximizing informal learning
Preparatory events on a shoestring
Achieving change via e-learning

Chapter 9—Designing Instruction: Foundations

Turning to instructional events, we look at foundations that have in many ways become more ritual and stylized than insightful and substantive. Looking at interactive events from the perspective of their four primary components has helped many instructional designers successfully transfer their skills from other media to e-learning. They are introduced here and taken up in much more detail in later chapters.

Major topics include:

Backgrounding
Iterative design
    Writing objectives that are useful
    Uses for objectives
    Working into objectives
    (rather than starting with them)
    Objectives x treatments matrix
Design challenges
    Page-turning
    Overdesigning
    Real instructional interactivity
The fabulous four
    Context
    Challenge
    Activity
    Feedback

Chapter 10—Designing Instruction: Meaningful Events

If a learning event isn't meaningful, it's a waste of time for the learner. This chapter discusses practical techniques to make learning events meaningful without having to develop multiple versions to accommodate variations in learner readiness.

Major topics include:

Success-based design
    Meaningful context
    Meaningful challenge
    Meaningful activity
    Meaningful feedback
    Where to start?
Meaningful learning events and instructional theories

Chapter 11—Designing Instruction: Memorable Events

If a learning event isn't memorable, it won't be able to influence behavior for long. Because success isn't just a good score on a posttest, but rather sustained performance excellence, we look in this chapter at ways to make learning events memorable.

Major topics include:

Teaching versus preaching
Success-based design
    Memorable context
    Memorable challenge
    Memorable activity
    Memorable feedback
Memorable learning events and instructional theories

Chapter 12—Designing Instruction: Motivational Events

Motivation is critical to both learning and performance. It may, in fact, be the most important behavioral factor we must deal with as designers. Without motivation, learners neither learn nor improve their performance. With high levels of motivation, people manage to learn and outperform others, although they do so more easily with the aid of well-designed learning events.

In this chapter, we discuss how to design e-learning that heightens motivation.

Major topics include:

Motivation is a prime target
Success-based design
    Seven magic keys
    Learning from games
    Motivational context
    Motivational challenge
    Motivational activity
    Motivational learning events and
instructional theories

Chapter 13—Designing Performance Aids

When performance needs internalized skills rather than just checklists or real-time performance prompts as provided by Electronic Performance Support Systems (EPSS), there usually is a need to help learners make the transition from learning environments to application. During this transition period, new skills are vulnerable to transmutation or extinction. Techniques for assuring successful transference are reviewed.

Major topics include:

It's all about performance
The performance phase
    Training supervisors
    Mentoring
Basing evaluation on observed performance
Encouraging self-testing
Teaching safety nets
Providing refresher events and practice
Applying behavioral change techniques
Blended learning

8 | Designing Pre-Instructional Events

Ichiro has varying levels of success with e-learning at Water Mountain Beverage Company, although his best successes have been with projects he had doubts about.

If you remember

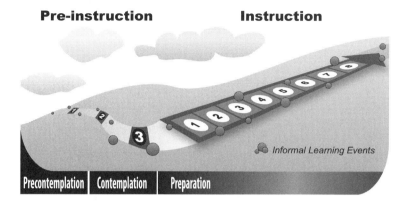

Pre-instruction   **Instruction**

Informal Learning Events

Precontemplation | **Contemplation** | **Preparation**

from Scenario 2, Ichiro prefers the expedience and control of designing and developing projects with minimal involvement of people outside his team. "After all, personnel supervisors

aren't instructional designers," he says.

When he's concerned about a project, however, Ichiro gets others involved in the process, especially at the start. And although he finds it tedious, the group support generated there probably has more to do with the success his applications have than anything else does. External support builds and churns up an enthusiastic and reassuring environment for learners, even before the learning starts. People are talking with great anticipation about upcoming changes long before enabling e-learning programs are released.

Potent preludes

In this chapter, we look at the possibility of dramatically increasing the impact of learning programs by designing events that prepare learners to truly benefit from the instruction to come later. This is more than providing a list of objectives and hoping learners will read them. For example, in advance of instruction, we can provide learners:

➤ Useful information about the advantages of improved performance.

Яapid readeR

- Change is difficult.

- Meaningful behavioral change rarely occurs just from distributing information.

- A change campaign creates momentum.

- Pre-instruction techniques can engage learner emotions and foster commitment.

- Informal learning can help (or hinder) change.

➢ Opportunities to make self-assessments about readiness, capabilities, and the benefits of new skills and behaviors.

➢ Personal and confidential advice, perhaps from learners who have recently completed the process.

➢ Ways to make a commitment public.

➢ Assistance in moving through Precontemplation, Contemplation, and Preparation stages.

There are many benefits to helping learners determine the value of performance improvements, commit to reaching performance targets, and make plans to learn and practice. Among them are more highly motivated and focused learners who are ready to take advantage of learning opportunities—the people who can make almost any instructional application work.

> **Think**
>
> What level of effectiveness is appropriate to sacrifice in order to develop e-learning faster?

Big stuff

I think this is big stuff. Really big stuff. Not necessarily costly or complicated, as we'll see later, but very big stuff for the e-learning designer.

But it's a change for us. And as we know, change isn't easy.

Almost since the Internet introduced e-learning possibilities to the masses, organizations have been looking for the magic key, the quick fix to overcome the one lingering, big-cost item: designing good learning experiences that are affordable to build.

Some feel we just have to do e-learning faster (the rapid e-learning crowd); sacrifice a bit of engagement if you need to, but get applications out fast. Some feel reusable objects are the answer; sacrifice design integrity a bit if you need to, but reduce costs through creating small instructional assets that can be arranged and rearranged to create multiple instructional events. Some feel that templates are the solution; sacrifice flexibility a bit if you need to, but empower subject-matter experts to create learning applications directly by selecting prefabricated interactions and inserting their content.

The bandwagon notion is that we simply have to make e-learning less expensive to design and develop. We have to create it faster, and, by the way, it has to be done by people with scanty instructional design expertise. *Cheap. Fast. Easy.*

Might as well add another descriptor. *Worthless.*

Cut the budget

Things we admire, things that work, things that have lasting value—all are typically crafted of inspiration and talent. If, on the other hand, you don't care about the effectiveness of a training application and don't intend to measure it, then cost, effort, and development time naturally become your focus. *If I make it look good, get it done fast, and come in under budget, management will think I did a good job. And if I make it entertaining and short, learners will give me high marks.*

Executives display their skepticism about the value of training every time they cut the training budget. To me, making cuts often appears rational because so many training programs do lack the ability to produce needed behaviors. They look good, have objectives, pretests, posttests, some clever interactive mechanisms—all the turkey stuffing and trimmings—but they achieve little learning impact. A cut in ineffective programs causes little pain and underwrites the executives' skepticism. It suggests deeper cuts might be in order.

Even instructional designers may subconsciously share in the skepticism and lower their standards. *Our training only gets people started, while the real proficiency develops on the job. We can just do something basic and make it appealing. What's really important is that we do it fast.*

Achieving impact

Cost, talent, and development time are always concerns, but if you seriously set out to improve performance, *impact* becomes your first concern. The proper perspective often seems to get lost. Consider this question:

What is a reasonable amount to spend for an e-learning program?

A) $50,000
B) $220,000
C) 5% of improved financial performance
D) Nothing

Correct answers:

D—if the program doesn't have measurable impact; ineffective programs pretty much waste the total investment and are a costly frivolity for any organization.

C—is certainly a good answer, although conservative; imagine making 1900% on your investment!

That's what you would make if you only invested 5% of the improvement you achieved. The absolute amount can range from a small figure, say $15,000 to millions. It's usually far more than is necessary to create a hugely effective e-learning program, but also far more than organizations allot.

Unfortunately, the typical answer given looks something like A or B, where an amount is determined simply by setting forth a budget number that seems like a reasonable and affordable cost. The instructional team is then charged to build a solution to fit within it. The funding may be too much or too little. If too little, it can easily generate a project that has no impact, become a total waste, and, ironically, be unaffordable. The unspoken expectation in simply spending a convenient amount (and also not bothering to measure the impact) is that while the training might do some good, it probably won't even begin to pay for itself. So one should enter into a learning project ready to accept it as a sunk cost? With typical designs, probably.

Since many learning programs do not, in fact, lead to performance improvement but simply placate someone's notion that training needs (unfortunately) be provided, the above reasoning actually does make some sense. Training is so often developed just because it makes sense to do so, or because employees will complain if it doesn't exist. *They'll also complain about the training, of course—everyone complains about training; but at least we'll have something for them to work with.* Until learning programs can be depended on to deliver real impact, we will continue to see numbers pulled out of thin air and having little justification or basis in need.

So what's the big excitement here? It's the notion that we may be able to design e-learning programs that are certain to be effective—or at least far more so than most are now. It's the notion that e-learning effectiveness is determined as much by what happens *before* and *after* instruction as by what happens *during* instruction. This discovery may be the long-lost key to high impact learning, or at least one of the keys we need.

In this chapter and those that follow, we'll discuss some exciting things—different things, infrequently done things—that instructional designers can do to create high-impact learning programs.

Change is difficult

Lack of success is inevitably traced to people not doing the right things at the right times. Individuals are often aware that things could be better, particularly in large organizations, but they don't so often feel that problems stem from their own behavior. When people have convinced themselves that the problems are rooted elsewhere, individuals don't take the initiative to change.

To make corrections or improve what people are doing requires behavioral change. And change can be difficult.

We know change can be difficult, and now there's physiological evidence to explain the brain's reluctance to change (Rock and Schwartz, 2006; Koch, 2006). Explained as briefly as possible, change or even just the prospect of change engages areas of the brain that consume high levels of energy. Instead of running idle, letting lower brain centers work in familiar patterns, change alerts and excites the prefrontal cortex. This can be pleasant and construc-

tive. Working at optimum levels, the prefrontal cortex teams with the amygdala, the center of the brain that's important for visual learning and memory, so that learning and effective decision making can occur.

But the prefrontal cortex is easily stressed and overloaded. When the circuit breaker pops from too much excitement or concern, the prefrontal cortex again enlists aid from the amygdala, which is also (here's the kicker) associated with feelings of fear and aggression. Now in a defensive mode, the brain works to escape unfamiliar circumstances, return to easy running, and cool off. Even if the escape is to old familiar behaviors that are known to be undesirable, the brain has protected itself, relaxed, and cast off the pain of the unfamiliar. It accepts the trade-off.

Resources

⌨ Rock, D. and Schwartz, J. The neuroscience of leadership. Downloaded on Oct. 16, 2006, from www.strategy-business.com/press/freearticle/06207?tid=230&pg=all

⌨ Koch, C. (2006). The new science of change. *CIO Magazine*. Downloaded on Oct. 10, 2006, from http://www.cio.com/archive/091506/change.html

Just the prospect of change, even a small behavioral change, can be enough to trigger the process.

There we have it. A physiological explanation of why people so often fail to do the right things at the right times, even when they know what to do. Knowing what to do and being comfortable doing it are just very different things.

Pre-instruction   **Instruction**

Informal Learning Events

Precontemplation	Contemplation	Preparation

Raise Consciousness ——————•
Facilitate Social Liberation ————————————→
          Encourage Self-Reevaluation ————•
          Engage Emotions ———————•
               Foster Commitment ——————→

Facilitating change

Knowing a bit about how the brain both accommodates and resists change, we can help learners avoid becoming fearful and defensive. We need to provide this help before we throw them into the pool, of course, and hope they will somehow conquer their fears and learn to swim

before they drown. That's why, way up front in the process, before learners have entered into instructional activities focused on new content and skills, we have important work to do—work that's so important it may determine the effectiveness of the entire learning initiative.

As discussed earlier and represented in the figure on the left, the Pre-instruction phase overlaps fully with Prochaska's first two stages of change, Precontemplation and Contemplation, and partially with Preparation. Prochaska identifies five techniques that various approaches to facilitating change have found useful during these stages. These techniques, together with a possible application in learning programs, are:

1. **Raise consciousness.** Raise the learner's consciousness about why personal change is important.

2. **Facilitate social liberation.** Provide a context in which the exploration of change, before making a commitment to it, is not only permissible but also encouraged.

3. **Encourage self-reevaluation.** Help learners put things in perspective and take manage-

able doses of risk, by helping them evaluate their current situation, how they feel now, and how they would feel if they became more proficient performers.

4. **Engage emotions.** Help learners energize themselves, by exciting them about the many levels of rewards successful behaviors can return.

5. **Foster commitment.** Help learners make a sincere and realistic commitment to seeing the learning and change process through.

Raising learner consciousness

To have an interest in learning and changing, people need to be aware of the effects of their current behavior or lack of response. In the Precontemplation stage, learners may be quite unaware that their behavior is a problem for anyone. They may be in denial about their responsibility and also be quite resistant to the notion that they should change.

Helping learners may first involve getting their attention, revealing the effects of their behaviors, and then helping them assess whether personal behavioral change would be beneficial to themselves or others.

When helping Precontemplators move to the next stage, it's important not to push them into action, nag, or minimize their responsibility for problems. Rather, we would like, as much as possible, for learners to initiate and own their program of change. As Koch says, "There is one aspect of change that scientists believe generates pleasurable sensations: the epiphany—that moment of personal insight when people feel they personally have come to terms with an issue" (2006, sidebar).

Perhaps the best and most practical approach to deal with all the change-facilitating tasks we have as instructional designers and get our consciousness-raising efforts moving forward with the involvement of all learners is through launching an organization-wide campaign.

The campaign

Consider setting up a campaign context for your initiative to affect change. A campaign for change can become a powerful context to get attention, gather support, and build inertia. Borrow concepts from successful advertising and marketing programs in which a clear message and vision are implanted in peoples' minds. If lottery promotions can get people to buy tickets that have almost zero chance of returning any benefit, you can get a program going that has much higher prospects of personal benefit.

The message

There is amazing power in the right message. A message can change national sentiments, inspire people to greatness, and even revise history (Ok, we don't need to go there). As we think about e-learning applications, how many had a well-defined message that captured the intent of the program or inspired learners to change? Most programs simply have titles that sound like this:

➢ New Global Employee Orientation (required)
➢ Documenting Programming Requirements
➢ The ACME Sales Process
➢ Our Management Practices 101

Inspired? Obviously, we'd like to provide as many moments of epiphany as we can for each learner. These dreadful titles aren't a good start in that direction. It's hard to feel much attraction, let alone enthusiasm. *The ACME Sales Process! Do I have to?*

Effective messages have motivational energy. They are aligned with the organization's culture and have credibility. They are, as all effective things in learning, meaningful and memorable. They relate to the individual and yet they also lend a vision of magnitude and success for the organization. Examples:

➢ Secrets You Should Know for Success and Power at Global
➢ Becoming Our Company's Most Loved Programmer:

➢ Easy Ways to Talk with Technology Idiots
➢ Doubling Your Bonuses While Clobbering Our Competition:
➢ A Two-Year ACME Initiative to Move Up to Number 3!
➢ Reducing Your e-Mail 40% and Other Cool Management Insights

Creating the message

Ideally, everyone involved in the program would participate in creating the message. It would be their message and become their initiative much more than if it were just handed to them. But this wouldn't be a very practical approach in most organizations. And if it could be done once, it could be impractical to repeat the process, potentially creating a new theme and message as each new learner came along.

But this impracticality doesn't mean that you shouldn't involve representatives of those people whose behavior you are setting out to change. You want your campaign's message to be something that connects to your audience and creates personal impetus for change. It's more likely you'll find an effective message if, just as advertising agencies do, you involve members of your target audience in the process of creating and evaluating different messages.

Organize a team and *ask questions.* Perhaps more than any technique identified in the literature, launching change initiatives that win both broad based and individual ownership involves asking questions. For example:

➤ *Ask some two- and three-year employees:* Why do you think people are confused about our vacation policies?

➤ *Ask some programmers and people who use programming services*: Why do you think our programmers feel no one appreciates them?

➤ *Ask a group that represents the entire organization well:* How do you think we can beat our primary competitors?

➤ *Ask a representative group of managers:* Why do you suppose none of our managers are improving their skills?

Note that we didn't start out asking what the campaign message should be. We start by drawing awareness to the behavioral changes that need to be made. Then, with some creative brainstorming and leadership, the group can grapple with the task of coming up with a campaign message that will spark the initiative. They'll begin thinking of supportive events, t-shirt slogans, competitions and awards. They'll smile, maybe even laugh. They'll see this can be fun, sense the prospect of real change, and anticipate the rewards of success. This is what you want.

TIP: Your own group of e-learning designers may need to revitalize itself to begin doing things of much more interest and impact. Question yourselves as to what needs to change and work toward a thematic message you could use to launch your own improvement campaign.

Marketing the message

You've got to get the message out for it to have impact. This is truly internal marketing and marketing that's well worth the effort.

What would you do to market any campaign internally? You would create imagery, slogans, and intrigue. You would attempt to set expectations that something great is going to happen and that one would be missing out if he or she didn't participate. You'd look for ways to make sure everyone saw this as real, serious, and important. And you'd look for ways to get everyone seeing how it can be fun, easy (or at least worth the effort), and rewarding.

Although there is no limit to the creative approaches you might identify, here's a checklist of some ideas:

➤ Mail promotional DVDs to employee homes.

➤ Set up a tradeshow-style booth and/or exhibits in the cafeteria or main hallways.

➤ Have a root beer float break with a senior corporate officer (who might not normally be accessible) to express personal enthusiasm and discuss the program openly.

➤ Set up competition between departments to see who can achieve the goals first.

➤ Use a Wiki to provide information, solicit suggestions, and report accomplishments.

➤ Create a hall of fame, with a picture plaque recognizing each person who achieves targeted performance levels.

➤ Hand out campaign buttons (caps, t-shirts, visors, etc.) and award prizes at random for people seen wearing them.

➤ Use different colored buttons to recognize individual levels of advancement. Again give random prizes for people spotted sporting their achievement buttons, giving more valuable prizes to those having achieved more advanced levels.

➤ Put thematic screen savers on workstations.

Start things off grand

Whether your program is ongoing or periodic, find a way to gather attention and help people make a public commitment. Start off with a grand event (even if it's something that's grand only in the eyes of the single individual starting the program this week) that says, *what's starting here is important.*

➢ Get some recent graduates together to give the "new kid(s)" some recognition and encouragement.

➢ Hang a sign announcing by name all of the people who are starting the program today. Balloons and cookies?

➢ Get the division vice president to come by and talk gratefully about how the program is designed by employees for the benefit of employees (only if it really is).

➢ Stream video interviews with each or a selected sample of the people who are starting the program today, including their individual hopes and expectations.

Keep momentum high

While a great start is a great start, it's important to keep the visibility, enthusiasm, and overall momentum strong. Plan events to reinforce the program as learners progress through it.

➢ Display progress boards in public places and/or electronically.

➢ Schedule individual learners or groups to demonstrate new abilities on preset dates.

➢ Have advancing learners mentor learners behind them (requiring advance learners to stay ahead).

➢ Change banners as teams make progress to indicate what phase each group is currently in.

➢ If there are any accumulating results from the program, such as increased revenue, academic papers accepted for publication, or decreased manufacturing accidents—whatever the target of the learning program is—publicize and celebrate them.

Create a marketing plan

Whether your campaign is large scale or in support of a small project, it's smart to think the program through as seriously as you plan your e-learning application design and development projects. Create a written plan, even if it's only several pages long. See the sample marketing plan outline on the next page.

Sample Marketing Plan For A Change Campaign

1. Analyze the Situation
a. Determine who owns the responsibility for change.
b. Find out what is the real purpose of the change and what are all the consequences of both achieving it and not achieving it.
c. Find out if change will be measured and if the results can be publicized (and when).
d. Look for political sensitivities. (Does everyone support the change? Is this change good for everyone? Could it be?)

2. Set SMART Objectives
a. **S**pecific objectives lay out precisely what you intend to achieve.
b. **M**easurable objectives allow you to quantify your progress.
c. **A**chievable, **R**ealistic objectives are the only ones that help; don't try for too much.
d. **T**imed objectives make your plan executable.

3. Involve the Target Market
a. Find out how people feel about making changes to their behaviors. Do they agree change would be good? Do some agree and some disagree? Have they tried to make these changes before? If so, what happened?
b. Select a representative group and have them brainstorm marketing tactics. (This can help make sure your program will relate well to your target market's lifestyle, values, and so on.)

4. Map Your Tactics
a. Set a schedule of events, mixing media, repeating core messages, and also keeping things fresh with surprising additions as you go along.
b. Get prices and adjust as necessary.
c. Determine who will be responsible for what.

Adapted from
www.marketingteacher.com/Lessons/lesson_marketing_plan.htm

Facilitating social liberation

One of the things that holds us back from making behavioral improvements, or changes of almost any sort, is the way others perceive us and the way we perceive others perceiving us. Even if we don't like how others see us, there's comfort in familiar ways of interacting, in familiar expectations and in familiar behaviors. And we can be entrapped by them. *Larry, think about it. In your first date, you can pretty much be anyone you want to be. In your second date, if you're lucky enough to have one, you need to be that same person again.*

Changing any of the behaviors that are familiar to you and to others you see frequently risks discomfort and possible embarrassment. It easily overloads the frontal cortex, enlists the amygdala, and triggers the flight response. In other words, changing behavior patterns easily elicits social discomfort, even when changes are intended to be beneficial.

Encouragement from others is helpful in many ways, but perhaps it's most helpful in that it gives us the means of changing our behavior with reduced risk of disapproval or awkwardness. In giving encouragement, people imply pre-acceptance of the change, giving us a preview of the new ways they expect to view us and respond.

The risk isn't gone, of course. Even when people express their encouragement, they can, and often do, disapprove when change happens. They don't think about the changes they might have to make in response, and when the change becomes necessary, they're faced with the same discomforting process themselves. *She was so much fun when she was an executive assistant who always screwed up, but now that she's taken that time management course we recommended, she's organized, punctual, and on top of her game. She makes the rest of us look bad.*

If behavioral changes require people to learn new skills, additional social risks come from the potential failure to learn the new skills and humiliation from mistakes made in attempting to apply them. *Bill's been trying to learn and use our CRM system for months, and it's clear now why he just kept putting it off. I don't think he'll ever be very good at working with online systems. And I always thought he was so smart, too.*

No learning program alone should be expected to reface the complex social environment of the workplace to provide optimal support for change, but some activities and events can help make the environment more conducive to change. A social environment that's favorable to change is one in which everyone is pursuing his or her own improvement and encouraging the efforts of others. An energetic focus on improvement can sweep reluctant changers along and help them feel a sense of belonging. It can reduce fears when it's recognized that no one is perfect and everyone can improve. Failures can be forgiven easily when an all-out effort is being made to improve.

In general, the more ongoing discussion about change, the more change-supportive the environment is likely to be. So one way to facilitate social liberation is to encourage group discussion. Another is to encourage informal learning. Some ideas:

➤ Have periodic discussions about change. What changes have we made and what have been the effects? What changes do we need to make? What should we be able to achieve?

> Set up a Wiki to chronicle attempts to make changes and the results of those efforts. Encourage personal anecdotes.

> Encourage people to post questions about learning opportunities and respond to them publicly.

> Set aside time for informal learning. Provide chat rooms and areas, both electronic and physical.

> Provide access to experts and/or people who have successfully adopted new behaviors.

Encouraging self-reevaluation

Just as we cannot learn for our learners, we cannot make meaningful commitments for them. Making

changes first requires personal readiness. The question as instructional designers is, *How can we help people ready themselves, make a commitment, and follow through?*

Ask questions

Since changers must reflect on themselves, the situation, and possible courses of action, and since people in general tend to push back when being told what they must do, the answer again appears to be asking

questions rather than giving direction or making suggestions—at least initially. Personal conversation prior to instruction may well be worth the effort, whether done face-to-face, on the phone, or via the Internet.

Try asking these questions, not so much to get answers as to get potential changers to reevaluate their readiness and decisions—to take a helpful look at themselves:

> How do you feel about your current performance? (Refer to the specific area of change being targeted.)

> How you think your performance could be improved?

> What do you think would happen if your performance improved?

Self-reevaluation through e-learning

One of our clients was developing state-mandated training for managers on preventing sexual harassment and properly handling sexual harassment concerns. They wanted excellent, highly engaging e-learning that truly fulfilled their obligation as a large-scale employer, despite the fact that much of the required content was deathly boring regulatory law and corporate policy. It needed to provide an energetic, upbeat experience because their managers didn't think they needed this training.

As the team talked, built rapid design prototypes, and evaluated them using the successive approximation approach, they created a fascinating simulation for the final learning event that brought together all the skills that one needs to competently handle harassment situations. It either confirms the learner's abilities to perform effectively or points out performance problems that need to be corrected, whichever is appropriate for the learner. It's actually a simple but fascinating simulation.

As we were looking over our nearly completed design, I was reflecting on a discussion we had about the employee's managers feeling they didn't need training on sexual harassment. They felt they had both the common sense and the experience necessary to comply with the law, to appropriately apply corporate policy, and to handle situations effectively and sensitively.

But with all the complexity in the policies and regulations, and the personal and emotional sensitivity of harassment situations, it was clear that managers couldn't possibly be as

skilled and prepared as they judged themselves. How could the company get enthusiastic participation? By encouraging self-reevaluation.

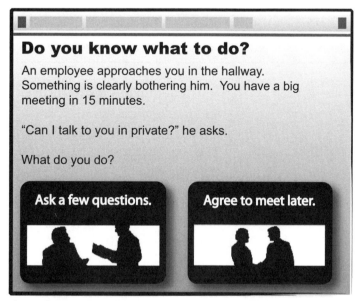

This e-learning application begins with simple scenario-based questions that few people answer correctly without training. It demonstrates the need for learning in a personal and private way.

The program was scheduled to roll out on a tight schedule. Completion of training by managers was a legal requirement and a prerequisite to continued employment as a manager. Much inertia was already driving this program, learners ready or not, and there were thousands of learners to be reached in many diverse locations. Yet, if the stages of change model is robust and learners must go through the stages to reach the desired change, the challenge was finding a way to help learners overcome their defensive and disinterested stance, and eagerly engage in learning and preparation to change their behavior.

The solution: Put the final challenge simulation up-front.

The solution: put the final challenge simulation up-front. Our client's first response was, "They'll all fail to make the right choices and be frustrated. That can't be good."

I agreed, felt stalemated, and then caught myself. She was right; most managers would fail to handle simulated harassment situations on the first try, and they would be frustrated.

But wait. *That would be good.* Managers would see quickly that they did need training. Not only would they fail to make the right choices (anyone would without being very familiar with regulations and policies), the simulation would also point out how damaging bad decisions can be. If the simulation situations were believable, and this was critical, they would convince managers that they didn't

know it all. Hopefully, it would also increase their interest in improving their skills.

The employer pushed back a bit. *But won't we get calls, complaining that they couldn't solve the simulation's problems?*

"So, you think your managers will flood you with calls to report that they really need training? I don't think so," I said. With plenty of help to learn the required skills, and now intrigued if not highly motivated, managers would be able to explore their strengths and weaknesses privately as they practiced new, effective behaviors. I'm happy to report that this is exactly what happened.

Engaging emotions

We can often rationalize with some ease those decisions made emotionally, but it's hard to reverse emotional sentiments, even when they're at odds with solid logic. If we let our emotions lead the way, we're more likely to get moving sooner than if we depend on logical analysis to remove all doubt. Getting learner emotions pointed in the right direction is therefore a helpful way to get moving in the right direction. Charging learner emotions may be the most important design task. Perhaps you can even get your learners daydreaming about the rewards their new proficiencies will return.

Here are a few ideas to help get your creative ideas flowing:

➤ **Set up competitive teams.** Although it may be hard for individuals to decide to change their behavior for their own good, being part of a group that's trying to become the best performance team in the organization can create excitement and a determination that wasn't there before.

➤ **Use role playing.** If you have some good actors in your midst, or at least some willing amateurs, see if they can create interactions with learners that have emotional power: a sick phone customer whose phone service suddenly started blocking outgoing calls, a machine operator whose boss picks on him, a clerk who cannot get the hang of the company's accounting systems.

➤ **Create a multimedia presentation.** Use the emotive power of music, animation, and a strong story to communicate the personal impact of successful behaviors and/or the dramatic consequences of ineffective behaviors.

➤ **Film a "jaywalking" segment.** Interview employees to reveal how oblivious some are to what they should be doing and to the impact of their behaviors. Or interview customers to find out how they've been treated and how they feel about it.

Fostering commitment

A major milestone in the change process is making a personal commitment. Commitment is a combination of confidence and readiness. It means holding anxieties in check, feeling that with determination you can succeed, and being ready to handle unexpected challenges.

Assess learner anxiety and help learners mitigate it if it appears too high. This can be done in many ways, including through interactive events that privately allow learners to gauge their level of anxiety, trace the source of their fears, and identify things that might help reduce it.

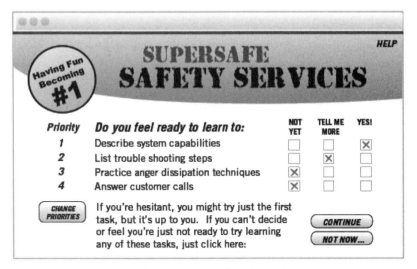

Fostering Commitment Through e-Learning Interactions

Suggest commitment to just a few small steps at first, selecting actions that are of lowest risk, and setting a date for specific actions to be completed. As confidence increases, you can help learners commit to greater levels of change.

To maximize commitment, have learners rank the importance of learning outcomes and performance improvement against other concurrent goals they may have. Hopefully, if proposed changes do, indeed, have significant potential value for the learner, the value of the learning outcomes will rank high among other goals they have.

Commitments to a vague course of action cannot be strong commitments. They lead to mid-process quandaries and provide dangerous wiggle room. So have learners set personal goals, make a realistic plan they can commit to, and share this plan as publicly as makes sense.

Planning activities should ask learners to consider the steps they think would be best and whether each step is acceptable and doable. If plans fail to meet these criteria, alternate plans need to be identified. As manageable steps begin to define a workable process, learners will hopefully convince themselves that they can succeed and make the necessary arrangements to do so.

Since making learning plans can sound like a daunting task and may, in fact, generate more dread than the actual learning tasks and changes under consideration, make the planning process as easy as possible. You might, for example, offer several different plans for selection and modification. It would be great if these plans could be plans generated and actually used by previous learners. Just knowing that other learners made and used the plans can help subsequent learners feel they aren't alone, even with their hesitations and uncertainties. And this can help them overcome fears and make a commitment.

Maximizing informal learning

In the Pre-instruction phase, learners can use the help of others to prepare for learning and ready themselves for change. They will find it useful to talk both with those who have successfully changed and with those who are also in the Precontemplation, Contemplation, and Preparation stages.

Talking with those who have succeeded in changing their behaviors, learners can:

➤ Set fears aside by discovering that some challenges aren't as difficult as they expect.

➤ Gain confidence by learning about successful approaches to challenges they hadn't considered.

➤ Find out that others who have succeeded had similar self-appraisals and doubted their ability to triumph over perceived weaknesses.

Talking with those who are in the same stages of change, learners can:

➤ Make plans to support each other.

➤ Discuss alternative plans and perhaps work out some teaming approaches.

➤ Identify information that would be helpful and decide how to obtain it.

Learnscaping

Jay Cross defines the term *learnscaping* as "removing obstacles, seeding communities, increasing bandwidth, encouraging conversation, and growing networks" (2006a, illustration). The insight here is that while informal learning has a certain unpredictability about it, there are things that can be done to increase the probability of it happening and also the quality and effectiveness of it when it does.

Some of the possibilities that derive from Cross's (2006b) observations of informal learning include:

➤ **Providing accessible e-mail and instant messaging services during work.** While we used to think of the organization providing the team from whom workers draw knowledge, inspiration, and support, the new generation of workers carry their work team with them from employer to employer. While, chatting can fritter away more time than the benefit provides, trustworthy employees can become much more productive with the support of their virtual team.

➤ **Posting physical discussion boards.** Collective brain mapping can stimulate productive thinking, while strategically placed whiteboards can provide a place for groups to congregate for short think-on-your-feet discussions.

➤ **Having bag lunch get togethers.** People generally relax when discussions are over something to eat. This can be an excellent time for important questions to be asked and answered in a comfortable manner. Providing writable table signs headed TODAY, I'D LIKE TO TALK ABOUT… and footed with, PLEASE JOIN ME! can help people comfortably instigate discussions. As Jay says, "Conversations are the stem cells of learning, for they both create and transmit knowledge."

Resources

Cross, J. (2006a). The Big (32") Picture of informal learning. Downloaded from http://www/jaycross.com/informal_bookposter.htm

Cross, J. (2006b). What is informal learning? Informal Learning Blog. Downloaded Nov. 2006 from http://informl.com/?page_id=580

Preparatory events on a shoestring

Preparatory events are invaluable for achieving behavioral change and can justify serious design and development effort. The rewards in terms of business success can easily justify the expense. On the other hand, a big budget doesn't mean good instruction. Recall the highly creative television ads we see in support of major programming events. Big budget. We often remember the creativity, but can't recall the product or sponsor the ad was created to promote. Bad advertising. Many people can remember they took training, but can't remember a single thing from it. Bad design, regardless of the budget.

There are two ways to look at this. First, effective change management programs can return millions of dollars of benefit to large organizations, whether through top line growth or cost reduction. Effective change can mean the difference between competitive success and failure or even financial ruin.

With this understanding, why wouldn't organizations fund performance improvement projects at healthy levels? Probably 10 percent of the expected impact would be enough to do so, and it would often be more than is needed.

The answer, of course, is that they don't believe the training program will achieve the performance changes needed and return large levels of benefit. And they often don't, to be honest. They rarely cover all the bases necessary to work people through the stages of change, build transferable skills, and nurture those nascent skills through to effective application. But they can, and when they do, they're worth far more than 10 percent.

If you're fortunate enough to have a strong budget, it's important that you spend it on those things that will make a difference. Here's where it's important to forget many of the things you've probably been taught about instructional design and do something interesting. Be sure to include pre-instructional preparatory events as you focus on behavioral change.

The second view is to realize that through confronting challenges with an effective design, big changes can happen. Even with a restrictive budget, you can achieve a lot more than designers who focus on content presentation and learner testing, exhausting their budgets on the least

Is 10% too much? Ask a budget maker for 10% of the return. They will look at a potential $10 million reduction, say in poor product returns, realize 10% is $1 million, and decide that's far to much to spend on any training program. They'll then budget a "reasonable" $60,000 (and pretty much waste it all because it's far too little and never recognize their loss). Wouldn't you invest $10 to make $100? I would.

effective aspects of performance interventions. Talented designers know how to apportion budgets so that they get the most bang for their buck. Experience and creativity can do a lot more with a limited budget than the unaware can do with a large one, but once again, it will probably be necessary to take a different approach than you've been taught.

Many of the things we are talking about in this book can be done with very little expense. Commandeering a whiteboard or two can sometimes be accomplished with a simple request. Posting some banners can likewise be a very inexpensive way to raise the organization's consciousness about a campaign to improve performance. Creating some interactions to help learners think about their goals is far less expensive than creating most instructional interactions.

Forget It!

Establishing a Theme and Change Campaign Logo

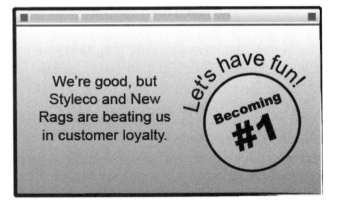

Promoting a Sense of Community Involvement (Social Liberation)

Achieving change via e-learning

Sometimes, however, attempting to do anything outside the design of interactive applications requires crossing an organizational boundary and perhaps inciting paralyzing repercussions. *You're the training department. Just stick to the training, will you?*

While far from optimal, a lot can be done to help learners prepare for success and make behavioral changes entirely within interactive applications. Instead of focusing initially on the development of new behaviors, which many of your learners may be far from committing to, you will instead begin by helping learners decide that learning and change are desirable—not just generally, but for themselves, individually and personally. You will resist plunging ahead with traditional design work in hopes of getting learners to make a sincere commitment to change sometime later, somewhere along the way. You'll work to make sure it happens when it needs to.

The screen sketches on these pages indicate some things you can develop.

Summary

There will always be pressure to reduce the budget for learning and training until 1) it is looked at as an investment rather than a cost and 2) decision makers have confidence that the investment will provide healthy returns. There's really no doubt that a proficient workforce is the means to profitability and/or organizational success, but there's plenty of doubt about what e-learning applications actually achieve.

Doubt regarding e-learning is well founded. We wouldn't see so many organizations adopting e-learning if it weren't reducing costs. And because perhaps as much as 80 percent of organizational learning happens informally, cutting investments in formal learning programs doesn't have much negative consequence. But the flip side is that e-learning can return invaluable results, the industry just hasn't been delivering them.

The results organizations care about are manifested in improved performance, and that requires behavioral change. Unfortunately, change is difficult. Fortunately, there are ways to design e-learning to achieve behavioral change, but this requires changing what we do as

Assisting with Self-Reevaluation and Planning

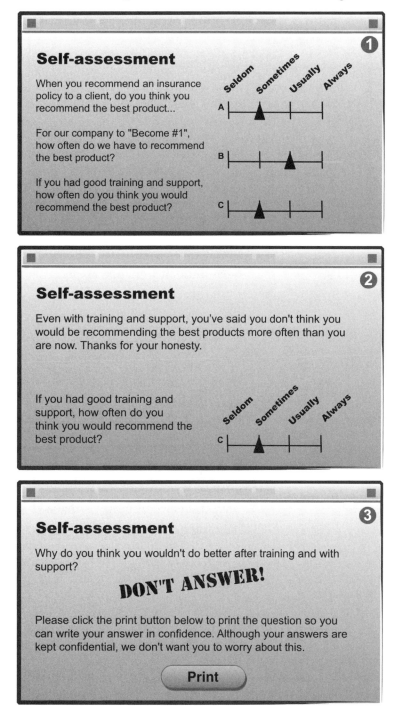

Fostering Support Groups

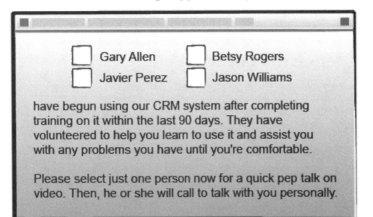

Gary Allen   Betsy Rogers
Javier Perez   Jason Williams

have begun using our CRM system after completing training on it within the last 90 days. They have volunteered to help you learn to use it and assist you with any problems you have until you're comfortable.

Please select just one person now for a quick pep talk on video. Then, he or she will call to talk with you personally.

instructional designers. And this can be as difficult a change as any.

In this chapter we reviewed the design of Pre-instructional activities—activities that have rarely been the province of learning programs, but are now seen to have much to do with the overall success of any learning intervention. By enhancing informal learning and helping learners through specific preparations for change, we can have far more impact on learners when more formalized learning events take place.

The Prochaska Stages of Change model defines Precontemplation and Contemplation stages through which learners should advance before formal learning begins. The Preparation stage should also be entered into. Techniques to help learners work through these stages include raising consciousness, facilitating social liberations, encouraging self-reevaluation, engaging emotions, and fostering commitment. Ways to implement these techniques in full or in part through e-learning are reviewed.

While there is some complexity and much to do to prepare learners for learning and change, this isn't necessarily an expensive undertaking nor unmanageable. It may be a necessary undertaking, however, necessary to achieve desired performance improvements.

9 | Designing Instruction: Foundations

We turn now to functions more traditionally performed by instructional designers, but we do so with no less of an interest in breaking down barriers that have prevented learning experiences from producing needed behavioral improvements and having measurable impact. Determined as we are to set aside those things that have had an unsuccessful track record, we must replace them with effective approaches. Thankfully, by borrowing

Forget It!

from the wisdom upon which alternative theories are based and upon the experience of successful designers, we have much to guide us.

So, prepare to forget what you know about instructional design and do something interesting—interesting to your learners, interesting to your organization, and interesting to you!

Design foundations

In this chapter, we look at the initial design tasks that create a foundation for all the remaining design work. As with building a house, creating a good foundation is paramount. It limits what can be done in subsequent development and influences many design decisions to come.

Foundational activities covered in this chapter include:

> Backgrounding—determining the fundamental needs and opportunities, including who the project stakeholders are and what behaviors need to be changed, if any

> Using prototypes to generate objectives

> Creating the objectives x treatments matrix

> Creating real instructional interactivity

> Using context, challenge, activity, and feedback to create powerful learning experiences

Backgrounding

Instructional design provides a creative problem-solving challenge to which many designers rally. But just as painters must carefully examine the surfaces to be painted in order

Яapid readeR

- Objectives need to be expressed in new ways to interest and motivate learners.

- The objectives x treatments matrix is a primary design tool that also helps reduce development costs.

- Context, challenge, activity, and feedback define the primary design components of interactive events.

to know what preparation will be necessary and select the right type of conditioner(s) and paint, designers need to patiently explore the problem to be solved before inventing solutions.

If approached with the right attitude, the process of information gathering can actually be as much fun as designing instructional events; but whether you relish it or not, it's important to learn all you *easily* can about 1) the problem you're trying to solve, 2) who cares about solving it, and 3) what is leading to the current problematic behaviors.

Doing your own investigation is important because it's very easy for organizations to misunderstand what is driving their own behaviors. Based on misconceptions, organizations rather easily embark on the development of training, which may be the wrong solution, and address either a non-problem or the wrong problem.

Please refer to *Creating Successful e-Learning—A Rapid System for Getting It Right First Time, Every Time,* the book immediately preceding this one in the library series, for details about backgrounding and discovering situational needs. As a quick reminder of the iterative successive approximation process, please review the diagram below.

Gathering background information is critical for making good use of the precious time invested in the Savvy Start design—prototype—review iterations.

I did say that during backgrounding, it's important to learn all you *easily* can. You shouldn't spend too much time and effort because the iterative process is a fast and efficient way to unearth root problems and get a good read on whether training is going to be an appropriate solution. On the other hand, you will waste precious time if the people

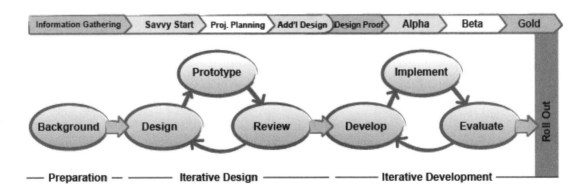

who can make decisions and provide essential information are not participating. So, work to learn all you can about the probable target audience, skills gap, and potential value to the organization of a performance solution, but worry most about whether you've identified the key people and convinced them to participate.

Key things to look for

When backgrounding, there are some primary questions to answer so that your design sessions can help determine what behavioral changes you need to achieve, what group(s) of people need to change their behaviors, and what blend of events and media can best accomplish all this.

Make sure there really is a human performance problem.

As obvious as it might seem, sometimes problems are caused by faulty equipment, lack of required tools, or inferior materials. It's important to know that improved human performance can make a positive difference before launching into a learning program with the intent of solving the problem.

Make sure the problem is caused by a lack of ability to perform.

When human performance is a problem, the underlying cause might not have anything to do with ability. For example, the poor performance may be caused by constraints imposed upon otherwise capable people. There may be systems in place or rules that cause problems to appear as inability to perform.

I worked once with a manufacturing team that wasn't able to consistently make their daily quota of shippable goods. Too many of the items failed to meet quality specs and had to be discarded. Management responded by ordering up a training program to teach workers how to maintain acceptable tolerances as they worked by performing quality checks throughout the process.

I discovered in talking with the crew, however, that the training wasn't going to make much, if any, difference. Why not? *We know how to perform the quality checks as fast as the measurement instrument can cycle. But it takes so much time, we can't make the quota when we do the checking, so we skip the interim checks and focus on making as many units as possible, hoping enough of them clear the final check to make quota. On our lucky days, they do, and everybody's happy!*

Perhaps the most common reason for lack of successful performance is not knowing what behaviors are desired. In many situations, people wish to perform well and will do so, even if they have to undertake extra effort to acquire the skills needed to do so. But misunderstanding expectations or misreading what constitutes desired behavior puts people on the wrong track. Sometimes, without knowing it, organizations reward behaviors that aren't desired. *If we slip out early, we don't have to stand around at the end of a hard day to listen to Pete tell us how great we are.* Before investing in a learning solution, see if you can eliminate punishments for good behaviors and rewards for bad behaviors. Make sure your target audience knows what behaviors you want and what the benefit will be to them personally for performing in that way.

There are often hidden punishments for doing things well. For example, who do you ask to take on another assignment if you want to be sure it's going to get done? Usually, it's smart to ask the busiest person around. That's because everyone asks the most reliable person to take on his or her tasks. Without meaning to, organizations often punish people for being great performers. Unless rewards outstrip the effects of punishment, expanding skills through learning programs isn't going to improve the situation.

Look for the determinants of behavior.

People do things for reasons. Their reasons may be built on misconceptions, fears and lack of confidence, desire to fit in and behave like everyone else, perceived strengths and weaknesses, and so on. To be successful with a learning intervention, instructional designers need to identify the primary determinants of the behaviors that need to be changed.

e-Learning is often an attractive behavioral intervention because it can offer individualized learning events to accommodate the variations in what is causing unsatisfactory behavior. The instructional designer cannot create effective individualization, however, unless

| **Think** | What are some reasons capable people might hide for not performing effectively? |

the operative influences have been identified. And since there may be cost considerations to individualize or personalize the instruction, this requirement needs to be known as soon as possible.

Iterative design

We covered the process of iterative design and prototyping in the preceding book of this library. We anchored the approach in the four components of interactive instruction (context, challenge, activity, and feedback) and discussed brainstorming approaches that are generally very effective. We also covered developing a matrix of objectives by treatments to be sure of having a complete solution. It allows us to economize by keeping the number of unique treatments to a minimum.

Here, as we review some of these key concepts, we also fill in some of the blanks relating to how instructional designers can help the team identify opportunities, narrow the vast array of possible solutions, and come to a consensus on designs that have a high probability of being successful.

Writing objectives that are useful

The *right* way to construct instructional objectives has been recapitulated, refined, and prescribed in so many texts and training manuals over so many years, it seems as though it must have been scribed when the Sumerian's invented cuneiforms and written language. *Proper* objective statements have three component requirements; they must: 1) describe observable performance to be exhibited under 2) specific conditions and to be performed 3) at a specified level of perfection.

These requirements emanate from actionable wisdom to be sure, ever since Robert Mager clarified the technique in 1962. Omitting any of the prescribed components makes objectives far less useful for declaring the intent of an instructional application and for measuring its success. But objectives that meet these requirements, however, are not always as useful as they could be. Audacious. Yes. It's time.

As Donald Clark (2006) put it in a recent interview, "Much e-learning is based on staid and outdated models... It's a shame that so many e-learning designers have gotten stuck in a rut." Regarding the mandatory

Things to Forget
Clark's Annotated List of Gagne's Nine "Dull" Commandments

1. **Gaining attention**
   Normally an overlong Flash animation or
   corporate intro; rarely an engaging interactive event.

2. **Stating the objective**
   Now bore the learner stupid with a list of
   learning objectives (really trainerspeak). Give the plot away and
   remind them of how really boring this course is going to be.

3. **Stimulating recall of prior learning**
   Can you think of the last time you sexually harassed someone?

4. **Presenting the stimulus**
   Is this a behaviorist I see before me?

5. **Providing learning guidance**
   We've finally got to some content.

6. **Eliciting performance**
   Multiple-choice questions, each with at least one really stupid
   option.

7. **Providing feedback**
   Yes/no, right/wrong, correct/incorrect…try again.

8. **Assessing performance**
   Use your short-term memory to choose options in the
   multiple-choice quiz.

9. **Enhancing retention and transfer to other contexts**
   Never happens! The course ends here, you're on your own mate….

Banal and dull
First, much of this is banal—get their attention, elicit performance, give
feedback, assess. It's also an instructional ladder that leads straight to
Dullsville, a straightjacket that strips away any sense of build and wonder,
almost guaranteed to bore more than enlighten. What other form of
presentation would give the game away at the start? Would you go to the
cinema and expect to hear the objectives of the film before you start? It's
time we moved on from this old and now dated theory using what we've
learnt about the brain and the clever use of media.

Blog downloaded 9/20/2006—
ahttp://donaldclarkplanb.blogspot.com/2006_09_01_donaldclarkplanb_
archive.html

listing of traditional objectives at the start of every course, for example, he said, "If that's your view, you don't deserve to be listened to. We know a lot about how the brain works: attention grabbing, cognitive overload, memory…but hardly any of that is taken seriously…instead the industry slavishly follows 50-year-old models."

I hold Clark in high regard for his willingness to speak out against dicta that, accepted as they may be in both literature and practice, have failed to produce energetic, fun, and effective e-learning. Granted, if such long-lived principles as Gagné's Nine Commandments (Gagné, 1965) were applied well, they would produce far better designs than today's average. But Gagne's principles and those of many venerable researchers and leaders (Bloom, Mager, Ausubel, and others) are quite frequently misunderstood and misapplied. The result, as Clark sharply observes (see sidebar), is that these principles seem to provide justification for boring designs rather than fostering the mesmerizing learning events today's technology allows and we all want. The point, of course, is not to follow guidelines but to produce compelling learning experiences.

Resources

Clark, D. (2006). e-Learning design can be better. *Newswire Today*. Downloaded from http://www.newswiretoday.com/news/8858/

Gagné, R.M. (1965). *The Conditions of Learning*. New York: Holt, Rinehart & Winston.

Mager, R.F. (1962). *Preparing Objectives for Programmed Instruction*. Belmont, CA: Fearon.

Mager, R.F. (1975). *Preparing Instructional Objectives*. Belmont, CA: Fearon.

Specifically regarding the commandment to precede instruction with objective statements, Clark asks, "What other form of presentation would give away the game at the start? Would you go to the cinema and expect to hear the objectives of the film before you start?" of course we don't think e-learning should be viewed as a presentation, but the point stands nevertheless.

Although gurus urge us to make objectives as simple and short as possible while including all three components, many designers are finding that longer objectives are more useful. Consider the example of a traditional objective that appears below. It is found in the second edition of Mager's *Preparing Instructional Objectives* (1975, p. 128) and purports to include all essential components:

Anatomy of a Traditional Objective

Objective Statement

Using any reference materials, be able to name correctly every item shown on each of twenty blueprints.

Components

Observable behavior:	correctly name items on blueprints
Performance conditions:	using any reference materials
Acceptable performance criterion:	correctly name every item shown on twenty blueprints

Good objective? Not really. It leaves important questions unanswered, and it would not serve well to guide the preparation of instructional events, just as it would not be effective as a motivator or preparatory aid for learners. For example, consider how important the following questions are and how many of them there are:

➢ Are the twenty blueprints of the same type or class of building (residential versus commercial, medical, or industrial, etc.)?

➢ Do the contents of the twenty blueprints represent all types of items any blueprint might have or just a selected set? If selected, what types of items are included and excluded?

➢ Were the blueprints designed in the last ten years, or do they include designs of historical interest?

➢ Are the reference materials to be located by learners or chosen from a set of materials made available; i.e., is selection of helpful and relevant materials a skill that is also being measured?

➢ How much time can learners take to answer?

➢ Are common names acceptable or are technical names required (or would a description of the item's function be acceptable)?

➢ What is the source of correct answers (and is it available for study)? Is correct spelling a criterion?

➢ Is there only one system of symbols, or are there multiple systems? (Which one is to be learned?)

Problematic is the lack of relevance this objective has to learners and the complete lack of context. Why should learners want to do this? Aren't legends or keys usually available, especially for rarely used symbols? How would names be used with clients, suppliers, regulators, and other architects? Is it item names that are important or an ability to read and discuss what the blueprint says that's important?

Regardless of all these things, where's the excitement, energy, and vision in this statement that's going to help learners learn? As an instructional objective, it poses more questions than it answers. By saying little about real-world relevance, it lacks power and interest.

Uses for objectives

Don't get me wrong. Objectives are extremely useful tools. They are useful as 1) design tools, 2) as a means of communicating the purpose of learning events to learners, 3) for evaluation of individual learner progress, and 4) for evaluation of learning applications as a whole. Because of the different uses, however, variations in the structure of objectives and language are necessary to create effective statements for each use.

Using objectives as design tools

Objectives to be used as design tools must provide enough detail about what will be learned so that stakeholders can agree among themselves that the design is complete and appropriate. Because it also matters how skills are developed, design objectives should provide guidance to content and application developers. Therefore, in addition to the traditional information expected in objective statements, objectives used as design tools should also:

➢ Be clear about why we are building each learning event. For example, is it to provide remediation, individualization, or person-alization? Is it to provide practice or generalization of skills?

➢ Explain how each learning event is to relate to other learning activities.

➢ Specify how the event will be meaningful, memorable, and motivational.

Using objectives to communicate with learners

We know from multiple areas of research that focus is important for learning. Some research has also indicated that careful reading of learning objectives enhances learning. But we also know from experience that few learners bother to read lists of objectives, let alone spend time fully absorbing them and setting their sights on appropriate targets prior to launching into learning activities. Objectives are important tools, but just as with two cans and a string, they won't communicate if they aren't used properly. Regardless of the potential value objectives hold for learners, if learners fail to read them, they will have little impact.

Perhaps one of the reasons learners opt to skip by lists of objectives is that the right way to write objectives has produced boring objectives. The standards for writing objectives haven't included the notion that objectives should incite curiosity, energize the senses, and build excitement. We see now, however, that objectives used as part of the learning experience should be written from the learner's perspective and help set up the pending learning experience. Consider constructing objectives that:

> Dramatize, in a believable way, the rewards previous learners have received from learning the skills covered.

> Present humorous attempts people have made trying to succeed without the necessary skills.

> Tell a story that takes the time necessary to relate to cynical learners and convey how valuable the prospective learning actually has been to those who made the necessary effort.

> Interactively ask learners to identify the consequences of behavioral improvement contrasted to the consequences of no behavioral change.

Note that objectives don't have to be conveyed in text, let alone as a single sentence. Possibly because brevity helps shorten the pain of plowing through them, the notion that an objective needs to be a single concise sentence has been instructional design dogmatism for far too many decades. Forget it! What's important is the impact objectives achieve, not so much the format in which they're delivered. Since achieving the desired impact is a challenge in it's own right, you don't need additional constraints to contend with. Write a story, present a video, or play a game. Do what you need to do. It's worth the time and effort. (See a sample objective on the next page.)

Using objectives to evaluate individual learner progress

One of the nice things about traditionally composed learning objectives is that they provide clear direction for determining success. By stating the performance to be observed, the conditions under which the performance must be given, and the criterion for successful performance, it's possible to set up evaluations that are unbiased and precise.

Instead of giving a grade or mark (such as A, B, C, D, F) or a percentile (such as *You did better than 76% of all students.*), objectives give the basis for giving meaningful feedback. *You have demonstrated that even with typical interference and distractions, you can retrieve a traveler's reservation record and explain all the options to reschedule travel dates and times.*

It's important to have good objectives to work with so that both learning events and assessment events coordinate to produce behaviors that can be measured and interpreted. Consider the following objective:

Given a typical office e-mail message that is 1) copied to too many people and 2) makes an unclear request that will require several subsequent e-mail exchanges to sort out, the learner will both identify these two faults and reconstruct the e-mail according to the preferred "action request" format and direct it to the appropriate person or persons. Students will be able to correctly identify all 6 problematic e-mail messages having these errors in a set of 10 and correct them within 40 minutes.

A Learning Objective Written For Learners

You are the new short order cook, and it's your first morning. An order comes in—pancakes and eggs with a side of bacon. You start the bacon, add the pancakes a minute later and finish with the eggs (sunny side up!). It all comes together beautifully on the plate, and goes out to the customer in record time. You think this isn't so hard—I can handle this!

The next order comes in, and it's three breakfast combos—a Denver omelet and an order of steak & eggs. This is a little trickier, and the omelet gets just a little bit cold waiting for the steak to finish, but still you think you've managed a pretty good showing.

Then you get an order for a 6-top (two combos, French toast, cheese omelet and two eggs Benedict with extra hash browns), and a moment later, three 2-Tops come in and you start to get a bit behind. Ten minutes later, you are backed up 12 orders, your pancakes are raw while the bacon is burnt, and the French toast is dried up. HELP!

AND HELP is here: You're about to learn the tricks professional chefs use to coordinate mixed orders, delivering them simultaneously with hot items hot and cold items cold, and all itmes cooked to perfection. Through practice in a simulated kitchen and some helpful on the job mentoring, you'll have the skills and confidence needed to succeed on your first day!

In this case, a set of ten e-mail messages needs to be presented to learners. Six messages must have the problem of both involving too many addressees and of making a request that would not be understood by the recipient intended to respond.

Learners would be expected to correctly identify the six problematic messages and correct them as taught in the course, all within a period of forty minutes.

There are, unfortunately, many questions left unanswered by this objective, such as:

> Are there different principles that determine who are the right people to receive an "action request" e-mail?

> Would it matter if the learner introduced other types of errors in making corrections?

> During assessment, can the learner look at all ten messages before identifying the problematic ones?

> Would it be acceptable if the learner misinterprets the action being requested but nevertheless writes a proper action request message directed to the appropriate person?

The lack of specificity may seem like a trivial annoyance until one sits down to design learning events or structure performance evaluations; then the need for clarity becomes acute. Consider the first question, for example. If there are different principles that determine the right people to address an "action request" to, can the "six problematic e-mail messages" represent all of the principles? Should they? If there are more than six, should a specific subset appear or a random subset?

The process of creating, reviewing, and reworking objective statements is useful for flushing out omissions and ambiguities and arriving at clearly defined performance measures. Ambiguities may not be detected until objectives are being scrutinized during the design of evaluation events. Unfortunately, if ambiguities are not discovered before learning events are constructed, there will be missing content and costly rework may be needed.

Enabling objectives versus terminal objectives

As we've seen, objectives are valuable for establishing requirements, communicating those requirements to developers, helping learners focus, and evaluating learner progress. Sometimes, however, objectives acquire a life of their own and are confused with the real target. Let me explain.

Think

Is it possible that the determination to create easily measured objectives have caused designers to stray away from teaching behaviors that matter?

Objectives are often tiered. Lower-level objectives that describe intermediate abilities that prepare learners to pursue higher-level objectives are called *enabling* objectives. In contrast, the ultimate objective that a training or educational program is designed to achieve is called a *terminal* objective.

For example, one could not likely reach sales quotas (terminal objective) without being able to make a convincing sales presentation (enabling objective), and one probably couldn't make a convincing sales presentation without knowing the attributes and benefits of the product (enabling objective). Enabling objectives are valuable in design work for identifying developmental and remedial learning activities that may be needed. They are also valuable in assessment activities for determining why a learner may be failing to reach higher levels of performance.

Too often, however, only enabling objectives are written for an instructional program because their corresponding behaviors are more easily assessed by quizzes and interactions embedded within learning programs. Dealing with only enabling objectives diminishes the ability of learning programs to achieve meaningful behavioral success. Enabling students to answer questions about how to drive a car, for example, wouldn't be mistaken for a competent drivers' education program unless the program continued on to the terminal objective of actually driving a car safely. But many instructional programs "terminate" with behaviors that are simply descriptive of the desired performance and therefore fail to yield needed value.

The target—the terminal objective—is to impart learners with the ability to perform real tasks with confidence. Don't let the convenience of measuring the enabling objectives prevent you from enabling your learners to achieve real-world success.

Using objectives to evaluate learning applications

Finally, because terminal objectives specify in detail exactly what the intervention is intended to do, they are a ready-made basis for determining whether an overall learning intervention has achieved what it was designed to do. As noted above and critical for this purpose, good terminal objectives state the desired real-world behaviors.

Don't confuse enabling objectives (even if they imitate proper terminal objectives):

> **Learners will be able to correctly identify 8 of 10 common blueprint symbols selected from *Building Codes Illustrated: A Guide to Understanding the 2006 International Building Code* (F.D.K. Ching and S. R. Winkel, 2006) within 20 minutes.**

with terminal objectives:

> **Learners will identify all structural code violations discoverable through a careful examination of blueprints and supporting documents. Ten cases will be drawn from actual construction applications submitted for approval in Hennepin County over the last 20 years. Learners may take up to one week to complete all cases, but must work without assistance. Case files will be opened one at a time and each opened case must be completed without leaving the examination room. Access to our reference library is permitted.**

Enabling objectives are useful for diagnostic purposes at *both* the learner and application levels. Measuring performance on them can diagnose where developmental weaknesses lie and explain why an individual learner is failing to reach targeted performance levels. Performed during the process of learning, testing on enabling objectives can determine where remediation may be needed. At the application level, measuring performance on enabling objectives can help locate weaknesses in application design that are causing learners difficulty and serving as a roadblock to success.

But remember, in no case should you celebrate success if you have only enabled learners to meet enabling objectives. Design success is at hand only if learners achieve the ability to perform at improved levels on tasks that matter. Making sure that you have a set of terminal objectives that truly represents the real-world performance you want to achieve will make them useful not only as design guidelines but also for overall evaluation that means something.

Working into objectives (rather than starting with them)

Because objectives can serve as design guidelines, it makes sense to write them early in the design process. First, define the overall goal of the project, then detail it by writing terminal objectives. Once they're in place, write enabling objectives that will help each learner achieve the terminal objectives.

Forget It!

Forget this!

While it does make intuitive sense to start with objectives, you'll find that path often leads to an ironclad recipe for doing something boring. Maybe it's just too much of a left-brain approach to produce the fun, engaging, and motivational experiences we need. Or maybe it's a design approach that prematurely focuses on closure.

The iterative process is powerful because it fosters brainstorming. It gets everyone looking at both the problem and possible solutions from multiple perspectives. Our successive approximation approach causes the project team to consider many possibilities repeatedly, and to be hesitant about settling on a possible direction before a broad range of designs has been considered. It even reexamines the goal iteratively, because the originally identified goal might, on closer examination, prove inappropriate for the project. It might be too broad or too narrow, too ambitious or too insignificant, focused on the wrong performers or not focused on enough. In other words, the process encourages being playful and messy before finalizing almost anything.

As prototypes are built and the team can see possible solutions in action, it's easier to assess the possible solutions they represent and answer the many concomitant questions. Having gone through this process with different teams many times, I can say with certainty that there comes a clear turning point when the group senses it is on to something that has high potential. The air becomes charged with expectations, and the group finds it easy, all of a sudden, to see many wonderful things that the approach enables and engenders.

The team may have changed the goal, changed the targeted behaviors, changed the targeted audience, and changed the instructional media to be incorporated. It's impossible to predict what will happen if the team is truly free to explore all the components of a successful project, but whatever the outcome, it really isn't helpful to substitute objective writing for creating prototypes. And it isn't helpful to write objectives prior to creating prototypes either, because the objectives only serve to preclude considerations. Rather, it is appropriate to draft objectives *after* the group literally sees a solution they are enthusiastic about.

Once you have a good collection of objectives, you will have seeded the objectives x treatments matrix and be ready to fill in the gaps and work toward a complete, well-organized set of useful objectives.

Objectives x treatments matrix

We know now how objectives should be constructed, what they are for, and when they should be written. Let's go just a bit further in the process to review the enormous value of the objectives x treatments matrix.

In order to minimize the cost of developing e-learning, we are constantly vigilant for synergies—those happy circumstances where one approach or solution applies to multiple needs. When a prototype defines a meaningful, memorable, and motivational event, the team has made a major accomplishment. But learning events are most effec-

tive when they build on a common context, reinforce each other, and use consistent conventions. It's important not to detail any single event too much before companion events have also been prototyped.

To do this is easy, in theory. To actually do this requires discipline.

Why is it so difficult? Good designs are rich with possibilities and offer almost endless enticements to explore them. Once you've centered on an approach, it's fun when you discover more potential in your ideas than you first saw. Stopping yourself and going on to other content areas that need to be developed requires the discipline to postpone this euphoric but potentially unending design work and tackle other needs.

It's very important to exercise the discipline to move on. If you don't and detail any event to a much greater detail than others, you will likely find the detailed event makes excessive demands on all the others, compromises how effective they can be, and decreases your freedom to create an optimal application. In going too deep before establishing the basic approach to all objectives, you may be specifying an unbalanced and suboptimal expenditure of your media and development

What would be some good techniques to be sure your design team doesn't design too much detail for one interactive episode before giving the entire application at least a "once over"?

resources, and you may not have discovered design synergies where one design can serve multiple purposes.

Constructing the matrix

As a tool for holding yourself back and maximizing the prospects for an optimal design, the objectives x treatments matrix makes design progress visual and plainly identifies remaining design needs for the entire team.

After you've built one or two prototypes around which the team is rallying, draw a simple matrix. Make columns for objectives. You won't know at this point how many objectives you'll have, so just plan to extend the matrix as necessary. Make a row or rows for the design treatment or treatments you have created. Again, you won't yet know how many treatments you'll need, so just plan to add rows as you go. Then, work backwards.

Working backward

Immediately, the group will begin to wonder how many behaviors, enabling and terminal, your designs will cover. Now, with prototypes in hand, you can think about those needs in fairly concrete and constructive terms. Prototypes will help

you see objectives you could easily have overlooked. They'll also help you see ways of clustering objectives that will be more interesting to learners than the ordering that's usually produced by analytical techniques. Although you still shouldn't worry about constructing complete objective statements, you can begin to flesh out the matrix and create a picture of the entire project.

If you've followed my advice to begin prototyping with behaviors that are close to the final behaviors you intend to produce, you've been working with terminal objectives or enabling objectives that lead directly to them. Among many helpful things this does, it helps your team reconfirm that the terminal objectives have been defined correctly and everyone is in agreement.

Make sure you create a column or columns for the terminal objective(s), enter them as column labels, and by using a different color or making extra heavy borders around the column head, make sure the terminal objective(s) are obvious.

Label the first row with the name or a short description of a design you've created (or selected). This is a treatment. If you've designed the foundation of additional events, add rows for each of them. Now place a checkmark in each matrix cell where a design is expected to lead learners to proficiency of the column's objective.

Working backward from the terminal objective(s), label a few additional columns with enabling objectives that appear necessary. You'll find it deceptively easy to do at this point, but go ahead anyway. Select some items to prototype and feel free to scratch out, split, combine, and otherwise modify objectives as your prototypes help you understand what you need to do. As you settle on designs, place checkmarks in cells where the treatments fulfill the needs of objectives. Sometimes, of course, multiple treatments are necessary to meet an objective, and you can easily indicate this by appropriately placing checkmarks.

Note: Try to prototype the "last lesson" early —the one intended to be taken just before learners complete their learning. My preference is to do it first. When you do, it's common to discover one or more undocumented steps of proficiency learners will need to be successful

performers. Objectives that were thought to be terminal objectives therefore become enabling objectives. No problem; this is a helpful adjustment. You may well find your team doing this several times.

Finding synergies

There can be very significant cost and time savings when a treatment has multiple uses and can serve multiple objectives. (We define a *treatment* as the basic instructional design into which different content can be inserted.) In addition, once learners become comfortable with a design and know how to work the interface, reuse of a design can make efficient use of learning time.

The objectives x treatments matrix not only identifies where synergies have been found, but can also help teams see opportunities to design multiple-use treatments purposely. Some caution needs to be exercised. Forcing broad utility on a treatment can easily dilute its impact and erode the fit between treatments and objectives such that no objective receives optimal learning support and all learning events are compromised. It's usually better to initially assume that a treatment will target only a single objective and to explore

> **Think**
>
> What is unique about e-learning, if anything, that makes effective instructional design so challenging?

later what might make the treatment effective for additional objectives.

Design challenges

In reflecting with talented e-learning designers about our disappointment that e-learning hasn't generally achieved a higher level of individual adaptation, fascinating interactivity, and skills transfer, I so often hear puzzlement about why designers "just don't get it." I think this isn't hubris speaking; it's truly lament and frustration. We'd all benefit from steadily rising quality in design and welcome widespread competitiveness on quality.

When you drill down to find out just what designers mean by the *it* in *they just don't get it*, I've found it was difficult for even the best designers to offer a definition. *It's all those things that go together to make a powerful learning experience.* Not very clear or helpful.

Capable designers, whether through intuition or schooling, feel they are generally able to recognize great design work when they see it. This is probably true, although I would assert that some designs are quite deceptive, and even experienced and knowledgeable designers can be misled.

Learners can be misled for a while too, but not for long. If a learning experience isn't working, learners usually sense that their time is being wasted. If the entertainment level is high, you can extend their patience, but lack of substance and benefit will be detected, and learners will abandon the application soon afterward.

Page-turning

Designers have become adept at disguising page-turning applications. Indeed, it seems that the subconscious agenda of many novice designers is to make page-turning palatable and somehow more than a presentation. *Click on each picture to review the product's features and benefits.* Page-turning. *Drag each tool to the workbench to see how it's used.* Page-turning. *Click any underlined term to see its definition.* Page-turning.

Now, techniques to manage display area confines and provide convenient access to information are helpful and good. The presence of these page-turning techniques does not incriminate a design. But these techniques do not convert a presentation of information into interactive learning. If only page-turning techniques are employed, the application is then simply a page-turner and a presentation.

Overdesigning

As you work iteratively and the inventive juices flow, you will be able to see opportunities to design interactive mechanisms everywhere. Your eagerness to design and build them may take you well beyond the needs of your learners, not to mention your resources. While much of today's e-learning fails because it is simply a glorified, electronic presentation of information rather than the learning experience people need, there are times when just making information available is enough.

The following table is helpful to be sure you're not creating more than you need or less:

Real instructional interactivity

Instructional interactivity can be defined as "Interaction that actively stimulates the learner's mind to do those things that improve ability and readiness to perform effectively" (Allen, 2003, p. 255). Genuine instructional activity causes rehearsal. Sometimes the rehearsal is only cognitive, with computer interface gestures serving as proxies for the relevant physical behaviors, such as adjusting the controls on a simulated lens grinding machine, taking eggs and bacon off a simu-

Presentations Versus Interactivity

Choose Presentations When...	Choose Interactivity When...
Content is readily understood by targeted learners	Learners are diverse in their ability to understand the content
Errors are harmless	Errors are injurious, costly, or difficult to remedy
Desired change to existing skill is minor and can be achieved without practice	Behavioral changes will require practice
Learners can easily differentiate between good and inadequate performance	Learners need guidance to differentiate between good and poor performance
Mentorship is inexpensive and will follow	Mentorship is costly, limited, or unavailable

lated griddle at just the right time, or "interviewing" job applicants by selecting the best question to ask. Sometimes, of course, the physical behaviors can be exactly the behaviors being taught, such as opening a spreadsheet file, filling out an electronic staffing requisition, or updating a medical chart. We know that the most effective training provides plenty of *authentic* practice—practice of the desired behaviors in the actual, or a very similar, context in which they will be performed.

Resource

📖 Allen, M.W. (2003). *Michael Allen's Guide to e-Learning.* Hoboken, NJ: John Wiley & Sons.

But even with a clear and understandable definition of instructional interactivity, the question of how to help designers "get it" remains. The answer, or at least a partial answer, lies in establishing a clearer conceptual framework and simpler vocabulary. While directives do exist in the volumes of research on human learning and instructional science, much of this wisdom is difficult for practitioners to interpret and apply.

Making it doubly difficult for designers are the gaps between research findings. We may never reach a point where sufficient research exists to answer every design question, but today, the gaps are sizable.

Finally, we have the challenge of generalizing findings that are only known to apply in specific circumstances. Most qualified designers become very uncomfortable when design recommendations claim to be based on research. Often, these designs are based only on *the assumption* that research findings hold true in conditions that differ from the conditions used in the research and are valid in the application at hand. Some findings may be robust and hold true across a broad array of conditions, while others may be true only under very specific conditions. Because we don't know which is which until appropriate research is done, generalization is risky business.

So then, what to do? To fill in the gaps and look for evidence of foundational principles, I've found it helpful to dissect e-learning of both highly successful design and ineffective design to see how the groups differ with each other and what the designs within each group have in common. Consistent with the success-based approach, designers can feel empowered when they know what seems to work in many situations and what rarely does. And what seems to help many e-learning designers is becoming aware of the four primary structures that define interactive events.

The fabulous four

Common among e-learning designs that reliably achieve desired impact is often, if not always, the inclusion of four carefully developed components: 1) context, 2) challenge, 3) activity, and 4) feedback. Further, how each of these components is developed contrasts with how they're used in ineffective designs, which commonly neglect one or more of these components completely.

The fabulous four are introduced briefly below. Later, we'll take them up again in detail as we consider how to employ each component to produce meaningful, memorable, and motivational learning experiences.

Context

Perhaps the greatest contrast between successful designs and unsuccessful ones is the development of a context. Contexts: two managers who refuse to cooperate, a faulty phone system, a diabetic refusing to monitor blood sugar, new employees needing orientation, an overwhelming number of complex products to sell.

There's a reason people say, *Let me put that in context for you.* Context provides the framework and conditions that make all things interesting and meaningful, including e-learning. It can make learning content relevant to the learner, it can get learners thinking about the applicability of what they are learning, and it allows you to give learners authentic challenges.

Challenge

The challenge is intended to stimulate the brain, cause it to scan information at hand both externally and in memory, and decide what action to take. The challenge is often made clear by instructions. *Stop the video when you see poor customer service occurring. Click all items that pose a health/safety risk. Calculate the amount of carpet needed to cover the area shown on the blueprint to be covered in commercial grade floor covering. Research the possible causes of poorly fitting vehicle doors, identify the*

Poor Contexts	**Better Contexts**
Poor contexts are general-purpose stages for question answering. They are totally unrelated to the content.	Better contexts provide authentic, content-relevant situations that learners can relate to and care about.
Examples	Examples
Academic style questions, tests, and quizzes, such as discrete, traditional multiple-choice questions	Simulated work environment, such as a restaurant, customer service counter, or a business meeting
Jeopardy, Who Wants to Be a Millionaire, or the $10,000 Pyramid game format, where the context is completely irrelevant to the instructional content	Task-focused environment that supports learner-relevant challenges and multi-step activities, such as a medical lab, an auto diagnostic center, or cell phone kiosk
Simulated classroom (as if somebody sees that as an attractive context) with chalkboard, teacher, library, etc.—again, content neutral	

Poor Challenges	**Better Challenges**
The weakest challenges are directions to "click here" or "do as I do." Slightly better, but still poor, are challenges that require only recognition of correct answers or recall of unprocessed information.	Better challenges are those that build on the context and require learners to consider various courses of action and select the best one.
Examples	Examples
Click NEXT when you are ready to go on. (There's *no* challenge unless you've hidden the NEXT button.)	Identify which paragraphs in the contract pose unacceptable risks to the client, and highlight the sentence(s) you would change.
Select the right answer to each (stand-alone) question.	Ask questions to determine ways the potential customer will use the phone, and then recommend two phones at different price points that should be of interest to that customer.
Read the material, then answer the comprehension questions.	

mostly likely causes, and select appropriate actions to remedy the problem.

Note that these example challenges are based on a meaningful context. Good instructional design links the four components together by building on the previous component and enabling the next. Challenges, therefore, build on the context and enable the learner to take meaningful actions.

Note: There are times when the primary task is memorization, such as the capitals of each U.S. state, the names of nerves in the body, or the prices of products. In these cases, a general-purpose context may suffice and the challenge may be as simple as recalling the correct information quickly. Unfortunately, many designers use this approach for almost all learning events. Even here, providing an interesting context can make the learning experience far more appealing.

Activity

Challenges call for action, and the actions learners take represent what they are thinking unless, of course, we've made it difficult for them to express what they were thinking. With e-learning, the actions learners can take are somewhat limited.

Most applications work only with keyboard and mouse input, which includes single-click, double-click, drag and drop, mouse-over, and the right-click variants. Voice commands and input are sometimes activated, as are touch-screen and additional devices.

The gestures recognized by computer overlap somewhat, but also differ considerably from behaviors human tutors can detect. Sometimes computers are better suited to evaluate activities. When teaching typing, for example, the computer can be flawless in detecting errors. More interestingly, the computer can detect slight latency variations for specific keys that no human would perceive; however, with this information, the computer can generate drills that will help typists overcome these slight behavioral deficiencies and perfect their performance.

On the other hand, most computers used for instruction are not well equipped to sense frustration, appreciate creative design, or evaluate a wide range of physical performances. Although technology is advancing rapidly, most e-learning applications are limited today to evaluating only the movements detected by the mouse and keyboard.

Poor Activities	**Better Activities**
Poor activities have great contrast between the gesture used in learning and the gesture used in actually performing the skill. They often burden the learner with remembering complicated interface rules.	Better activities feel natural and are similar if not identical to the movements one would make in performing the skill.
Examples	Examples
Having learners click the paragraph "that best describes the order in which you would mix the ingredients."	Allowing learners to drag ingredients to a mixing bowl in the proper order.
Having learners use the keyboard to type the pitch name (F#) and then type the value (e.g., sixteenth note). To place notes on a musical score, the learner must then type the number of the measure and then the beat after which to insert the note—followed by the return key, of course.	Allowing learners to drag musical notes of selected duration values directly to the score. Notes can then be dragged to different positions to make corrections easy.

It's really quite amazing what a little ingenuity in design can make of mouse and keyboard input. But it takes ingenuity and considerable design talent to avoid confusing learners and leading learners to make input errors that inaccurately represent their abilities. Just a little bias in the process can lead to frustrated learners and ineffective experiences.

We go into depth on learner interface design in another book in this library series, but you'll find primary guidance in remembering to design activities so that learners can readily communicate their think-ing and demonstrate their abilities. Minimize the likelihood of making errors that inaccurately represent the learner's intent, make guessing difficult, allow learners to make corrections and experiment with alternative answers, and minimize the effort it takes for learners to understand the input options available to them.

Feedback

There are many different ways to inform learners about the quality of their performance and their learning progress. *Extrinsic feedback* is perhaps the most frequent and least effective way. *That's right, Javier,* is an example of extrinsic feedback that may leave the learner quite bewildered as to what makes an answer correct or incorrect.

Instead of judging answers and telling learners that their answers are correct or incorrect, *intrinsic feedback* allows learners to see the effects of their answers and equips them to judge correctness themselves. The dough rises, the budget totals to the correct amount, the customer places a large order—all are examples of intrinsic feedback. Intrinsic feedback is the experienced designer's preference because it focuses the learner on successful performance rather than on winning approval.

Many of the significant things we learn to do are accomplished by making a series of choices and performing multiple tasks. As learners improve their skills and can begin to focus on the whole of a multi-step task, it's possible to rely heavily on intrinsic feedback and delay judgment further and further. By delaying judgment, interactive designs can provide learners the opportunity to observe the effects of their actions, make corrections (as we're often able to do in real life), and reach a desired goal even if initially through a somewhat circuitous route.

Poor Feedback	**Better Feedback**
Applies judgment criteria for the learner and reports the results immediately, depriving learners of becoming able to judge their own actions.	Better feedback helps learners see the effects of their actions.
Examples	Examples
That's incorrect. Try again.	The press foreman reports that the crew can handle your new schedule, but because paper stocks are low, two of the publications will be delayed.
You earned 16 of 20 possible points.	
The correct answer is B. Click CONTINUE to go on.	Your sales prospect is agreeable to a meeting, but has decided to seek competitive bids while waiting for you to schedule the meeting.

Summary

It's important to get off on the right foot when starting to design learning applications. In this chapter, we suggested doing things quite differently than has become tradition, such as working into the statement of learning objectives after the development of prototypes and writing longer objectives that communicate more fully about why specific abilities are important to learn and how they can be applied.

The perplexing issue of why many instructional designers fail to grasp the critical concepts of designing for interactive learning is reviewed, noting that while page-turning has it's place, disguised page-turning doesn't make it a more useful learning tool.

Essential and also helpful to designers feeling stymied by the desire to be creative, is focusing on the "Fabulous Four": context, challenge, activity, and feedback. Putting attention to these components helps designers see opportunities for powerful learning activities and stimulates creative thinking.

10 | Meaningful Events

Class begins. I'm seated in the front row, notebook open and waiting for sage inscription. I glance about with enthusiasm. This is a favorite subject of mine. The professor smiles at me as he begins his lecture, but my enthusiasm quickly turns to fear and panic. I have almost no comprehension of what the instructor is saying. Unfamiliar terms and concepts meaningless to me are tossed out to the grateful, head-nodding groupies surrounding me. Even the questions they volley back are babble in my ears. The professor turns and asks me an incomprehensible question. I awake sweating.

It hasn't happened to me often, but it has happened—*twice!* Once would be enough to generate the occasional nightmare. I was placed in an advanced college calculus class without ever having taken any previous calculus, and I did try to take an object-oriented programming class that was designed for top-level object-oriented programmers with years of experience (I had none at the time). These frightful events were both memorable (traumatic is closer to it) and motivational in a way (I now take precautions to avoid reliving such tortures). But two of the three M's, memorable and motivational, are not enough. Learning experiences must always be *meaningful* if they are to be successful.

In this chapter, we cover an instructional design approach that helps everyone, both novices and advanced designers, generate more creative designs that can also become very memorable learning experiences. We look at each component of interactive learning events—context, challenge, activity, and feedback—one at a time to discuss their roles in making events memorable.

Яapid readeR

- To have value, learning events must be meaningful.

- A meaningful context is powerful.

- Meaningful challenges and activities get learners practicing useful skills.

- Intrinsic feedback builds on context to be meaningful.

Success-based design

Success-based designers are constantly looking for ways to avoid fashioning boring and frustrating learning experiences. They look for every means to engage the learner and make such good use of the learner's time and energy that the learner stays engaged. The first step to avoid boredom and frustration, and to engage learners, is to be sure the learning event is meaningful.

Successful design techniques to make sure learning events are meaningful to each learner include:

➤ Using a context that relates to the learner's current situation or a situation and responsibility that learners expect to encounter

➤ Creating a compelling interest story that builds on a developed context and allows learners to select tasks of importance and relevance to them

➤ Basing each module or segment of instruction on learning skills that:

• Can earn learners recognition

• Look harder to do than they are (everybody likes to get in on tips and secrets)

• Are fun to do, yet valuable

➤ Providing sideline resources that explain terms, concepts, or procedures learners should know but may have forgotten or missed

➤ Providing browsing capabilities

As with other aspects of our design and development approach, iteration seems vital to creating an effective design rapidly and dealing with all the complexity at hand. Since feedback, activities, and challenges are based on context, it never works well to finalize the context before looking at the challenges that can arise from it. Similarly, it's a mistake to affix challenges before being sure there are measurable activities learners can perform and that meaningful feedback can be offered in response to variances in learner behavior.

But we have to start somewhere. I'm actually of the view that it doesn't matter much where within the four components one starts kicking out design ideas. Because they are so intertwined and because it requires iterations to get all of the components optimized and building on each other, I think it's fine to begin with any component that has, for whatever reason, sparked your imagination. I do have a recommendation, however, if nothing is tickling your fancy. But you'll have to wait until later in this chapter to learn what it is.

Let's look at how some of these techniques play out in application using the four components of interactivity to structure our view.

Meaningful Context

To make e-learning applications meaningful, we need to create a context to which learners can relate and within which they can find interest. Since context is the glue that holds all the design components together, it's worth putting in extra effort to get it right and develop it fully.

The context should:

➢ Be meaningful to the full range of targeted learners

➢ Stimulate curiosity, interest, and inquisitiveness

➢ Engage learners, perhaps through empathy or fascination

➢ Energize learners, perhaps by revealing an underlying risk

Obviously, a lot depends on the context, but there are many techniques that can be effective. Don't get the idea that effective contexts are expensive, time-consuming, difficult to create, or appropriate only for large-scale, high-end e-learning applications. Quite the contrary, good contexts are often simple ideas drawn from thinking about the actual contexts in which targeted learner behaviors will be performed. Consider:

Meaningful Context

➢ **A typical workplace of offices and cubicles** A bird's eye view and the opportunity to eavesdrop on what's going on are inherently interesting.

➢ **A doctor's office** Medical situations provide a stage for tension and drama.

➢ **A sales conversation at a tradeshow in which you can hear what the prospect is thinking in addition to saying** Sales attempts carry the risk of rejection, and developed well, risk gets attention and involvement. Having the magical ability to hear what people are thinking as you talk to them is fascinating.

➢ **A video stage set for a televised interview** The learner can be either the interviewer or the interviewee. Even obviously fake contexts can jump-start attention. The possibilities are truly endless.

Place and situation

Note that context usually has two components, a physical place and a situation. (See examples in the table below.)

A well-crafted situation is usually a conflict, problem, or opportunity and communicates something important. It tells learners what can happen and why learning the skills at hand has relevance. And by revealing a story, it avoids a boring lecture format.

Although it's usually the situation rather than the physical place that offers most of the impact, basing the context on a physical place that can be represented in display graphics or described with realism helps learners better prepare for real-world events.

They can then visualize events, their response, and the likely effect their response will have. Such mental rehearsal is valuable practice.

Keep number of contexts to a minimum

Not only does developing an interesting context strengthen the impact of learning activities, it also makes all your other design work go faster and more easily. It will suggest challenges and activities you might have overlooked when you were writing objectives. It will remind you of the interrelationships and complexities that real-world behaviors must contend with.

In addition, a good context can go a long way. It can serve a wide

Example Contexts

Physical Place	Situation
A manufacturing plant	Parts jamming up on conveyer belts
Flight deck of an airplane	Inexplicably losing altitude
Sales counter	Three people clamoring for your attention
Your computer screen	Your upset manager wanting you to straighten out some accounting
Commercial kitchen	Orders coming in faster and faster

range of learners, sometimes even serving those who have relatively meager to no skills all the way up to and including advanced performers. And it can be the backdrop for addressing a whole chain of learning objectives. You can always stretch the context, if you need to, by adding and subtracting elements as needed. A little evolution of the context can help keep it fresh and workable for more advanced learning objectives.

Building on a single context is also practical from a design and development cost point of view. Sticking to a single or small number of contexts concentrates your resources and should afford more highly articulated media development. In contrast, using many different contexts quickly dilutes available resources and restricts what can be done with them.

Consider the context of a burning building, for example. A storyline can be developed that involves uncertain information of whether there are occupants in the building and whether this building that had once housed flammable, pressurized liquids still has them.

Additional information can "arrive" from time to time to redirect focus to different learning objectives and yet allow the basic context to keep the design unified. In order to achieve individualization within a single context and thereby keep interactions meaningful for each learner, different challenges can be selected based on performance.

The power of context

Regardless of the learner's skill level at entry, a story developed on a theme such as a burning building can provide a sense of tension and urgency, which are memorable in their own right. Assuming you're a firefighter in training, this context provides relevancy across a broad range of skills and content areas, such as asbestos, electricity, architecture, flammable liquids, foam, firefighting apparatus, and emergency medical treatment. One set of graphics, perhaps with animation and sound, can set up the background for a strongly engaging, interactive learning experience.

Superfluous contexts

Let me underscore the importance of making the content relevant. It's not true that any context is good. I've seen crazy designs that might be called *mixed metaphors* (although *convoluted contexts* might be more apt), such as using the metaphor of trying to get an airplane off the ground to teach leadership, using a kitchen and recipe cards to teach people to use a data entry system, and using a train switchyard to teach time management.

While some of these unexpected design solutions evidence creative flair, it's usually a mistake to use a metaphorical context that's unrelated to the learner's performance arena. Sometimes it draws so much attention that it's quite counterproductive. For example, while there are specific procedures one must follow in order to complete tasks in a data entry system, which is indeed something like following the directions on a recipe card, the designer is going to have trouble making the cooking context relevant and comfortable for learners who are fretful at the stove. Additionally, there will be structures in the data entry system for which there are no apt parallels in a kitchen. The designer will waste a lot of time and effort trying to create conceptual connections and make them clear.

> **Think**
>
> Think of the e-learning applications you've taken. Remember the contexts? Did the better applications have better contexts?

Similarly, learners will waste time and energy learning the connections rather than learning data entry.

Edmond Manning, a talented instructional designer with whom I'm honored to work, likens context design to stage set design. He sees the context as the stage on which interactive events play out. "There should be nothing placed in the context that isn't helpful and meaningful to the learning process whether it contributes by making the context as realistic as possible or provides tools for learning," he says. The match is critical. You would not typically stage software engineering in the old west, just as you wouldn't stage employee orientation in a galaxy far far away (humorous as it might be). Fit the context to both your learners and to the learning objectives so it can be a useful tool rather than a fanciful diversion.

Common oversight

Probably more than other faults, weak e-learning designs consistently reveal a lack of relevant context. Without a workable context, it's much harder to create meaningful demonstrations and offer helpful information, let alone design effective challenges, activities, and feedback. Make sure you've got the right context. It's good practice for yourself and your learners.

Meaningful Challenge

Challenges continue the storyline begun in the context and ask learners to do something about or with the presented situation. There are primary opportunities to address meaningfulness in the design of challenges, but they are easily over-looked. Diagramming sentences, for example, may be an excellent task for examining sentence structure, but if it's a task set forth with no connection to a meaningful context, it's one of those abhorred *trust me, someday you'll be glad you know how to do this* things.

Since learning success depends on meaningfulness, it's imperative not to neglect making each challenge meaningful. To do this, success-based designers attempt to connect everything the learner does to the meaningfulness of the context place and situation; i.e. if the context presents a situation—whether conflict, problem, or opportunity—that the learner would like to address or at least recognizes as something that must be addressed, the task of creating meaningful challenges is off to a

good start. We can then help the learners create plans of action—*their* plans of action—that seem logical and meaningful to them. The plan of action is essentially a sequence of tasks to be learned, all focused on the contextual situation.

Working backward

It seems to me that so much of what one should forget about traditional instructional design approaches is the order in which design tasks are to be done and even the order in which we should have learners perform their learning tasks. Just as we espouse working backward from prototypes into objectives, for example, it also makes sense to have learners work backward in comparison to what is typical; viz. instead of working up from learning basic, inherently uninteresting skills to something with understandable utility, why not confront learners with meaningful tasks, however undoable they may be at first, and help them build the needed skill set?

We generally find the *tell and test* method (presenting a bunch of stuff then seeing if learners can recall it) to be far inferior to *test and tell*, in which we first let learners try a task (test) that's likely to be beyond their current abilities and then help them (tell) when they request assistance. Although this is an important and effective technique for maintaining learner motivation, it's also an invaluable way to keep things meaningful for learners. To be clear, the meaningfulness comes from seeing that the skills I'm acquiring as a learner are being acquired so that I can complete a higher-level task that I care about.

Meaningfulness ripples backward from the context into the highest-level performance skill(s) we are targeting, and from there down into each enabling skill. As long as we keep the connections clear and are willing to demonstrate when necessary how each task enables a valuable, higher-level one, we have a good chance that learners will see and feel that everything they are doing has meaning.

Individualization

The tasks given to an individual can vary with the known skill level and goals of the learner. For example, one learner's assignment might be to determine whether the burning building should be entered, and if so, where and when. The learner could tap various sources of information in making the decision, but you might not credit this learner with a correct answer if not all the pertinent sources of information had been tapped or if the learner took too long to decide. It would depend on the objective, of course.

Other learners might be given the challenge to make sure firefighters are properly dressed and equipped for this call. Some might be challenged to execute an interior fire attack properly, while still others might be required to execute an entire mission and rescue the elderly woman on an upper floor. Building on the context will help make the learning meaningful, but going further to adapt challenges to each learner's position, background, readiness to learn, and any other relevant factors takes the process an important step forward.

Selecting and sequencing challenges

There are multiple schools of thought as to whether the software or the learner should select and sequence challenges. Since adult learners usually want to have as much control as possible, there's a reasonable argument that at least adults should be allowed to take the responsibility and select for themselves. Others would argue that since learners are not expert in what they are studying, they couldn't parse the structure of complex skills and map an effective course for themselves.

Perhaps a third school of thought calling for a blend of the two approaches is the best resolution. It is, indeed, what has been successful in my work for many years. This approach can be called *mixed initiative*, to borrow a term from the field of intelligent tutoring systems.

With mixed initiative, the learner can exert control over what is happening, as can the software. If the learner is feeling frustrated by either too little challenge or too much, the learner can interrupt what's going on and redirect the interaction. Similarly, if the learner's performance is falling below baseline or indicating that the challenge level

Michael's Rant: In the 1970s, there was considerable interest in testing learners to determine their skills levels and also their learning styles so applications could provide matching instructional treatments. Although interactive learning events were more difficult and expensive to develop then than they are today, we had the notion that by amortizing development costs across large numbers of learners, we would be able to afford the development of multiple designs. Additionally, we thought branching techniques would allow fine-tuning of learning events for maximum effectiveness for each learner.

Today, instead of focusing on such powerfully individualized applications, there's considerable interest in dumbing down designs so that they can be built with minimal thought, time, and effort. Developing a single effective treatment seems almost beyond reach, let alone developing a half dozen to cover the same content in different ways. Surely the lack of effectiveness will catch up to these inane approaches and we'll get back to taking much more effective advantage of what learning technologies have to offer.

is too low, the software can make adjustments automatically or, usually better, ask the learner if adjustment would be acceptable.

Meaningful Activity

As a primary component of interactivity in e-learning, we define activity as the physical gestures learners make to communicate with the computer and, among other things, demonstrate to us what they can do. Behind the physical gestures, of course, is mental activity, which is actually becoming more and more directly measurable through the use

Meaningful Activity

of advanced technology. Although only a comfortable cap or wireless headset is necessary for some of these devices (see below), it may be a while before we begin working directly with brainwaves as learner responses and measures of abilities in most e-learning. Herein, we will look primarily at gestures performed with the computer mouse and keyboard and sometimes verbalizations picked up by microphone

Direct Measurement of Mental Activity

A currently available wireless system measures "the three principal dimensions of mental processing: focus, alertness, and awareness." The entire system can be mounted in a golf cap or visor.

Photo used with permission from: www.peakace.com

to represent cognitive and physical abilities.

Again, if the context, together with its place and situation, are meaningful, and if the challenges to the learner are meaningful, the activities that naturally fall out of these learning aids are likely to be meaningful as well. Let's review some of the characteristics of activities that can help make learning experiences as meaningful as possible.

Match activities to objectives

The first thing to do seems obvious: match the activity to the objective. For example, if the objective is to *recall* three-letter airport codes for U.S. cities, the activity should be naming the airport codes, probably by typing them or speaking them. It would be a mismatch to have students select them from a list, as that activity would be appropriate for an objective (perhaps an enabling objective) that called for *recognizing* the codes.

Similarly, if the objective is to assemble a toaster, the activity learners perform should be as close to assembling a toaster as possible. Gestures that the computer can recognize are limited, of course. Assembling a toaster isn't currently one of them. If practicable, a blended solution may be the best approach, wherein an expert would observe, evaluate, and perhaps mentor learners attempting to assemble toasters.

It can be difficult in many circumstances to arrange for an expert to be available when a learner needs a performance check or midstream mentoring. Staffing is probably the biggest problem. It could be that many learners need help at the same time when there wouldn't be enough experts available. On many other days, no learners may need observation or help. Experts might sometimes be supervising production lines in order to fulfill orders and meet deadlines. Learners may be in distant locations. And so on.

Approximating ideal activities

When it's not possible to have students perform ideal learning tasks as may be called out in objectives, it's usually possible to design activities that build competencies that are close to the targeted behaviors—so close, in fact, that learners may be able to make the final learning step easily. We're not talking about mismatched activities here, but rather activities that require learners

to practice essential thinking and visualization when fully performing the task is not feasible.

Consider toaster assembly again. Some mismatched activities would be naming the parts of a toaster, recognizing the electrical capacity of the power cord, or even describing toaster assembly. These diversions are often taken. Forget them. Appropriate approximated activities would include selecting photographs of toaster parts in the correct order for assembly, matching tools to the parts they are used to install, choosing the one video of a set of videos that shows proper assembly, and stopping a video of toaster assembly when a mistake is made.

Think

Think of a task performance that cannot be measured by typical e-learning computers, then list appropriate and inappropriate approximating activities that can be measured.

Visualization

You might not think of visualization when you think of activity, but the two are quite closely related. Let's start with an example.

The objective is to *identify the proper sequence of performing CPR.* We can have learners type step or sequence numbers beside each item as in the first two figures (next page).

Order CPR steps by typing the number 1 in the box beside the first step, 2 beside the second, and so on.

2 Blow through mouth

☐ Position hands between nipples

☐ Press down 1.5 to 2 inches

1 Call 911

Text-based Sequencing Activity

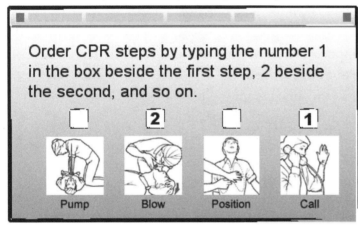

Order CPR steps by typing the number 1 in the box beside the first step, 2 beside the second, and so on.

☐   2   ☐   1

Pump   Blow   Position   Call

Text-based Sequencing Activity With Graphics

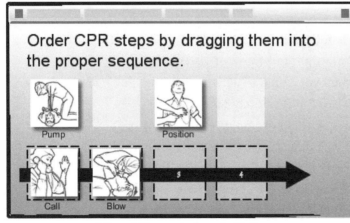

Order CPR steps by dragging them into the proper sequence.

Pump   Position

Call   Blow   3   4

Visual Sequencing Activity

This structure is found quite often in e-learning designs, but it deprives the learner of any helpful visualization. Lack of visualization is sometimes addressed by adding or substituting visual depictions of items to be sequenced while keeping the same user gestures (middle figure).

Unfortunately, this design only helps learners visualize the items to be sequenced and, as in the first design, fails to give the learner visualization of any sequence and especially of the correct sequence. Since the objective is focused on sequencing, both the visualization and the learner activity should emphasize ordering. One solution is to have learners move items into the proper sequence (bottom figure).

Moving items is a more memorable activity than typing numbers because it creates an image as you go. Learners focus on items as they move them into place, and focus on them again as they assess the fit between adjoining items. Further, the gesture of dragging items into place reinforces the importance of sequencing, while pressing keyboard keys relates poorly to the concept.

In general, think of click responses when dealing with selection and recognition, drag responses when dealing with sequencing, and typed or spoken responses when dealing with recall. There are exceptions, of course, so evaluate what the learners should be thinking as they perform tasks and chose gestures that reinforce proper thinking.

Authenticity and fidelity

To help learners focus on what's really important and to facilitate transfer of training to real-life behaviors, we want tasks to look and feel as realistic as possible. Provide controls, such as switches, levers, and knobs, that look and act like real controls learners will use. Similarly, if learners will have to type entries into forms, have them type those entries; don't have them drag words. If learners will mix chemicals in a beaker, have them open supply containers demonstrating safe ways to do so, use burettes or other appropriate devices to measure out quantities, and move through each step of the process so that they won't be confused when they get to actual laboratory work. Sometimes it's the simplest pragmatics that trip people up, so think of details and create the highest fidelity simulations you can.

Of course, all activities should fit the instructional objectives and strategy. We have noted that in order to maintain meaningfulness, it's usually best to focus initially on a task of interest—a real task for which there can be recognition and satisfaction. Then break the task down into subtasks to teach component skills.

So as not to immediately lose learners in details, you can and probably should "automate" some steps that learners have not yet learned to perform. You can gradually remove the automation as learners become more capable. If you can reveal how automated tasks are being done at the time they are being done, the demonstrations may both help learners understand their relevance and prepare learners for future learning.

Simplicity

Point and click has become synonymous with quick and easy. An interface is considered to be elegant and empowering when we can get what we want and expect with a single click.

The lesson for e-learning designers is that we must avoid unnecessary complications or our learners will turn on us, and rightly so. It's amazing how complicated we can make learner interfaces and sometimes do. It's very true that simplicity often takes extra work and reflects greater sophistication and design accomplishment than complex and confusing interfaces, but the first design requirement is to avoid distracting the learner from his or her attempts to learn.

Dragging is a gesture to be singled out because it's often misused. It may seem that dragging interactions are more sophisticated and therefore provide advantages over other gestures, but dragging is often unrelated to tasks it is used for and may defocus learners. It's not an easy gesture for many people to use. If a simple click works, it's probably the better choice. Do consider dragging activities, however, when:

➤ **Teaching concepts.** Consider having learners sort items into IS AN EXAMPLE OF and IS NOT AN EXAMPLE OF bins by dragging items to the appropriate location.

➤ **Teaching sequences.** Have learners drag items in order. If they omit an item or put one in the wrong place, give learners a simple way to make corrections; allow them to drag items to different positions and even shove one between others.

➤ **Teaching chronology.** It's similar to sequences, but spacing between items becomes significant. The visualization of this activity combined with cognitive judgment of the precise placement of items is important.

➤ **Teaching device assembly.** This is also similar to sequences, but when the learner places the right components next to each other, you can demonstrate how they are fitted together and perhaps show how subassemblies are created.

➤ **Teaching placement of items.** Cooking, laboratory work, spatial planning (arranging furniture, positioning troops, landscape design), and other situations where items are placed or brought together are examples where dragging reinforces thought.

➤ **Simulating controls.** If controls slide, be sure learners can drag the sliders. Note: dragging is a fairly effective way to simulate turning knobs, but *neither* the mouse or keyboard is particularly good at rotating knobs.

Exploration and experimentation

When we were designing Authorware®, a commercial authoring tool for creating interactive learning applications, it was clear to us that we had to focus *more* on allowing authors to make changes, corrections, and additions to developing structures than on initial creation tools. Authors made their initial entries only once, of course, but they often wanted to make many changes as their work progressed.

The need to allow learners to edit their work easily is just as important. Exploration and experimentation are powerful paths to deep learning. We've observed learners working through the same learning interactions repeatedly with different strategies. Often, the first time through, learners will do their best but make errors that reflect their incomplete skill levels. Opting to try it again, learners usually try to get through without error.

You might think that would be it; getting through with no errors or very few would signal completion and time to move on. But no. Many try one more time, and on this third pass, they intentionally make errors, lots of errors. Why? They wanted to see what happens when you really "mess things up." Realizing there was feedback that correct answers didn't reveal, learners wanted to see what they were missing.

Learners shouldn't miss the opportunity to explore and experiment because it's an unsupported activity. Consider allowing learners to submit multiple answers without penalty to see what happens. Consider also allowing learners to browse ahead and review. Why should e-learning applications be less pliable and user-friendly than a book? It takes extra development work to allow fluid navigation through an interactive application, but if this is a requirement set out at the beginning, it's often a reasonable thing to do.

Meaningful Feedback

We obviously want feedback to be meaningful. There are so many reasons why *intrinsic feedback* is to be preferred to *extrinsic feedback*, and this is one of them. Let me explain.

Intrinsic feedback is the result of an action taken. A manager fails to respond to complaints of sexual harassment, and a lawsuit is filed against both the manager and the company for which she works. A salesperson learns to listen constructively and her sales triple. A machine operator disconnects the danger alarm and loses a finger. That's intrinsic feedback (both in real life and in a simulated situation), and it tends to be memorable.

By contrast, extrinsic feedback is offered by a person or software and usually includes judgment. *You're doing excellent work, Michael.* This kind of feedback tells learners that their job is to please the source of the feedback—the teacher or the e-learning application. While it can work learners through a course of instruction, extrinsic feedback often fails to make clear the connection between different actions and their results. Learners come to know, *these are the answers he likes* while, for some reason that may not be at all clear to learners, *these are the answers he doesn't like.* Without understanding why some answers are correct and others aren't, critical meaning is lost.

The lesson here: Make your feedback intrinsic and it will be meaningful.

Meaningful Feedback

Where to start?

With an iterative process and components that all interrelate, a good question is where one should start the design process. As I said early in the chapter, it's fine to begin with any component, context, challenge, activity, or feedback that has, for whatever reason, sparked your imagination. But if nothing has and you're feeling a lack of direction—the creative inspiration just hasn't hit—then I suggest first choosing an activity for the learner to perform.

As I so frequently advocate working backwards, this is another one of those places you can start with the desired end result and work backward. Think of what you actually want learners to do, the most important thing you want them to do, after completing the instructional program. This is obviously a behavior you want learners to practice. So design an e-learning activity that has them doing that or something that's a close approximation of it.

Then I'd suggest devising the context in which you most often expect learners to perform within. Design that. Then create an appropriate challenge to illicit the desired behavior. And finally, design intrinsic feedback that will let learners see the consequences of their behaviors.

I know, activity, context, challenge, feedback might seem like an odd sequence. And I don't suggest this is mandatory or even preferable if another sequence works well for you. But if you feel lost or just need a little experience before you can develop your own preferences, this is a way to start.

Meaningful learning events and instructional theories

It's comforting to have supportive company in the principles I'm recommending to you. Many instructional theories advance principles that stress the importance of meaningful learning events. Below I have highlighted some of these key principles within some of the most influential theories along with the design principles that were discussed in this chapter.

To reiterate, successful design techniques to make sure learning events are meaningful to each learner include:

➢ Using a context that relates to the learner's current situation or a situation and responsibility that learners expect to encounter

➢ Creating a compelling interest story that builds on a developed context and allows learners to select tasks of importance and relevance to them

➢ Basing each module or segment of instruction on learning skills that have value recognized by learners

➢ Providing sideline resources that explain terms, concepts, or procedures learners should know but may have forgotten or missed

➢ Providing browsing capabilities

Very briefly bulleted below are correlating items from the mainstream design theories introduced in Chapter 5:

Cognitivism

➢ Make training problem-centered.

➢ Help learners assume control of their learning.

➢ Provide meaningful practice.

Constructivism

➢ Instruction must be concerned with the experiences and contexts that make the student willing and able to learn.

Minimalism

➤ Provide training on real tasks.

➤ Promote reasoning and improvising.

➤ Allow learners to read in any order. This requires, among other things, that text resources be complete and independent rather than requiring study of other resources for them to make sense.

➤ Use situations to make exercises meaningful and purposeful rather than structuring artificial tasks that require learning without context.

Merrill's First Principles of Instruction

➤ Learning is promoted when learners observe a demonstration.

➤ Learning is promoted when learners engage in a task-centered instructional strategy.

Summary

In this chapter, we cover a way to structure the creative process of designing meaningful learning envents. Meaningfulness is an imperative, lest the learning experience be totally unproductive for the learner.

Early work in e-learning attempted to provide elaborate ways

Resources

Alessi, S. and Trollip, S. (2001). *Multimedia for Learning: Methods and Development*, (3rd ed.) Needham Heights, MA: Allyn & Bacon.

Wilson, B.G., Jonassen, D.H., & Cole, P. (1993). Cognitive approaches to instructional design. In G. M. Piskurich (Ed.), *The ASTD Handbook of Instructional Technology* (pp. 21.1-21.22). New York: McGraw-Hill.

of testing individuals and placing them with regard to measured abilities at appropriate points within a fixed sequence of instructional events. We now find simpler ways to provide individualization that are quite effective and much less costly and complicated to design and build.

In this chapter, we began building adaptable learning events by defining a context that has interest to a wide range of learners. Learners take on challenges of meaning and interest to them, regardless of preparation level. If they need assistance, they dig down to the level of current proficiency and work up, always focusing on the achievement of interesting tasks.

Activities are given meaning by making them authentic; i.e. they replicate as close as possible the actual activities proficient performers perform. Feedback is intrinsic, coming in the form of results and consequences that learners can see and access for themselves, and is therefore meaningful.

11 | Memorable Events

Honey, on your way back from work today, would you please drop by the grocery store and get some milk, eggs, and an anniversary card for our neighbors, Ted and Mary.

Sure. No problem. See you later.

Honey, did you get the milk and eggs? Oh, man. Sorry, completely forgot and drove straight home. I'll go get them right now.

Thanks. Did you get the anniversary card? No. Forgot that too. Um, who was that card for again?

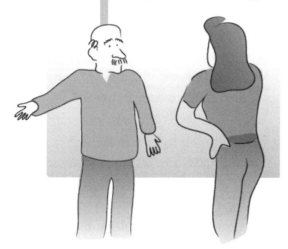

It's hard enough to remember what you need to do, let alone break familiar habits to do things a different way. With the continual bombardment of information we endure today and the need to adapt to changes almost constantly, our memories have a lot of trouble, particularly with new information and new behaviors that are not yet well ingrained and habitual. But if the skills we impart to learners don't survive long after training and if learners don't retain the ability to recognize when to perform what functions, then our learning events have come to naught.

Having looked in the previous chapter at ways to make learning experiences meaningful, we look in this chapter at ways to make them memorable.

Teaching versus preaching

For decades many (but certainly not all) teachers have acted on the assumption that presenting information to students is teaching. To make sure learners pay attention and actually learn, teachers threaten quizzes and final exams. And you know what? Students do exactly what teachers want: they learn to perform well on the exams.

We see this technique carried forward in many of today's e-learning designs. Literally moments ago, as I sat writing this chapter, I received an e-mail message from a company interested in hiring one of my studios to develop custom e-learning for them. In the request were the following words:

> We are looking to replace training which is currently being presented via in-person, PowerPoint presentations with interactive, self-paced instruction that could be completed at home by our trainees after attending four days of classroom training. We would want to incorporate visuals, evaluative questions, and a tracking system to determine completion of the course.

This request may represent a great opportunity, and I certainly hope it does, but I fear the buyer is looking for someone to convert existing slides to "interactive" e-learning by simply posting them on the Internet with narration or explanatory text, and then by adding some questions at the end to be sure learners "understood" and can regurgitate the information. The result, if this path is taken, will be that classroom time and associated costs are reduced, training is easier to manage, post-test scores are good and the same as before, and performance levels are pretty much the same as before. Overall, it will be seen as a success despite the fact that the training did little of the good it could have done.

If we human learners see our responsibility as doing well on tests, as indeed the tell-and-test framework implies, we adapt ourselves to exactly that task. We rehearse just enough to keep needed information and concepts in short-term memory to do well on the day of the exam. Then, with the task accomplished, we stop rehearsing and efficiently forget much of what we've learned almost instantly.

There are ways to set learners on a much better course and to help them retain and apply their learning where it counts—not on quizzes, of course—in the real world. It is the responsibility of the instructional designer to make this happen.

Success-based design

Success-based designers are focused on the learner's success. They know that success isn't achieved by simply knowing things or "doing well" during the course of instruction; it's what happens afterward that counts.

As a systematic method of designing high-impact learning experiences, we turn again to the four components of context, challenge, activity, and feedback. Successful design techniques for making sure learning events are memorable, and therefore able to serve the learner past the conclusion of instruction, include:

Context

➤ Using a strong storyline, perhaps with suspense, unusual circumstances, humor, or drama
➤ Employing fascinating media with unusual perspectives, imagery, sounds, and/or animation
➤ Providing imagery for concepts and/or performance consequences
➤ Providing mnemonics or having learners develop their own

Challenge

➤ Demonstrating successful techniques
➤ Showing learners how to apply a simplifying technique
➤ Allowing learners to do something they wouldn't ordinarily be able to do; e.g. if you were CEO of the company…
➤ Undertake bigger and bigger

challenges that require learners to apply more of their skills

Activity

➤ Having learners express what they've learned through different channels (describe it verbally, write it down, draw a picture of it, evaluate another's performance)
➤ Providing sufficient practice
➤ Spacing practice up to the point of matching the spacing that occurs on the job

Feedback

➤ Using intrinsic feedback
➤ Using strong imagery, and/or animation for specific correct and incorrect responses (bridge collapse; burnt bacon)
➤ Using drama and/or humor to demonstrate the disastrous effects of poor performance and/or the amazing consequences of great performance (happy postcard from a travel customer)

Let's look at how some of these techniques play out in application using the four components of interactivity to structure our view.

Memorable Context

Cognitive research reminds us of something that seems pretty obvious through a bit of introspection: that learning is a process that begins with attention and perception. New concepts and data points reside briefly in short-term memory, which evaporates quickly as yet more new information arrives.

To complete the process and keep new information from evaporating, we have to create a network of relationships to the new information and rehearse the use of that network in activities that require the recall of the new information. The associative network provides retrieval "handles," which are used to recall the new information. With use of the handles, the associative network strengthens and eventually secures a place for the new information in long-term memory.

In other words, learning requires 1) perception of new information, 2) making sense of it by associating it with current knowledge, and 3) practicing retrieval and application of the new knowledge. So, to get things started, we have to get the learner's attention and focus it on what matters.

Using a storyline

Stories are developed for the very reasons we try to develop strong contexts; they are devices intended to communicate and make their messages memorable. Techniques found in good story writing are therefore of great interest to us in instructional design, such as suspense, unusual circumstances, humor, and drama.

Stories usually have four primary components: a main character, a setting, a problem, and a resolution.

The main character

In e-learning, the main character can be the learner, and often is, but sometimes it's more effective to have the learner guide, protect, and make choices for a fictitious character. We've successfully used the approach of having learners guide another character when there are strong emotional feelings at stake, when we wanted our learners to look at issues from a different point of view than their own, and when we felt our learners were too close to an issue to think objectively.

For example, when working with children who had been bullied at school, we felt they could think more clearly about available options for dealing with the situation when they were "advising" other characters. When we wanted people in a manufacturing plant to change their routine, we had them "advise" people manufacturing different products but facing the same need to change.

The setting

To assure relevancy and meaningfulness, we often want the setting to be very close to the setting in which the learner will actually perform. Whether it's represented graphically, verbally, or both (which is usually best), we need learners to visualize new behaviors actually being applied in a realistic environment—an environment they expect to be in.

As with the main character, however, it's sometimes very effective to initially spring learners free from all those things that are personal and familiar, especially including those things reinforcing current behaviors. We may not actually know what all the effective factors are that keep people satisfied with their current behaviors, but there are usually

many. So if we're trying to change behaviors, it can help to take learners away from their current setting and present them with someone else's situation (everybody's situation always looks easier to contend with than our own) for a while. You might want to even give them almost a problem-free setting at first, just to help them figure out what would be ideal behavior in such a setting.

After working in someone else's shoes or on an idyllic planet, however, it will be important to introduce settings that are increasingly similar to the setting in which learners will actually be expected to perform. They may have to learn methods of dealing with objections, resistance, confusion, and other responses to change as part of managing their own ability to change.

The problem

We already talked about the importance of the situation as one of two components of the context.

> **Think**
> Can you think of a way to put your last e-learning experience into a story context?

161

Here we might introduce suspense, unusual thought-provoking circumstances, humor, and/or drama. For example, vodka mixed with soft drinks has been found in your work area and it appears that one of your employees has been drinking on the job. Another example: Restricted high-tech information has been distributed abroad by your company and federal orders have been issued for you to determine the extent of the offense.

The storyline problem sets up the big challenge for the learner. And the challenge, of course, may actually represent many component challenges. Basing the instructional design on a storyline can really speed instructional design and simplify the task, but perhaps more importantly, stories have been used as an effective way of keeping information alive down through generations. And it has worked. We don't usually set such a grand goal for ourselves, but we would like our learners to remember what we've taught them for a useful period of time. Stories work.

Now, don't think your content just has no story potential or that stories wouldn't work for your learners. Stories aren't necessarily long,

complex, and involved things. Think of a very short story, such as *Mabel, a customer of yours, recommended your company to a friend. Now she discovers her friend received very poor treatment, and Mabel is embarrassed. She wants to know why this happened, what she can say to her friend, and how you're going to make things right.*

Sure, but you're thinking, *We're just teaching our people to use a new project tracking system. They've just got to put the numbers in the right places at the right times.* Do you really think there isn't powerful story potential here?

The resolution

Like the punch line to a joke, the resolution carries a lot of impact and often serves as the "handle" for remembering the whole joke. Since we're very concerned about memorability here, bring your story to an end with punch. Your learners might not all be promoted to CEO because of their extraordinary post-training performance, but maybe they can dream a little.

Bring your stories full circle—back to the beginning—and contrast the initial situation to what it's like now. Your learners have new competencies and hopefully new confidence in their ability to perform as well. Perhaps you let learners choose an ending to the story they like best or write their own. Or, perhaps you surprise them by presenting a problem they wouldn't realize they can now solve and letting them demonstrate their abilities to themselves.

Memorable media

There are times when media jolts the senses and injects an image or concept, together with emotional and cognitive associations, into long-term memory quicker than a dentist can fill a cavity (a process that also injects a memory quite effectively). We've used the animation of a crashing plane in an e-learning application, and no one who has seen it forgets it. There's an e-learning application that visualizes the Doppler effect, complete with synchronized sounds. Just watch it once, and you understand the Doppler effect. No narration or verbal explanation is needed.

But use of memorable media for instructional purposes, especially in e-learning, is tricky. Every artist wants justification to play with all the powerful graphics and animation tools we have today and the opportunity to create dazzling eye

candy. All those people who feel video is the solution to everything are now joined by newcomers who, now seeing sufficiently high fidelity video playback capabilities on the Internet, cannot wait to victimize learners with hours of talking heads. *Instructional design? Why? Just let me tell learners what they need to know.*

It sometimes feels like there are few of us to stand against the mob, but it is very easy to contract a case of media mania and waste precious development resources on media that have little value. The situation is actually worse than this, because many of the fascinating things we can do with media actually detract from learning outcomes. For example, as Lowe (2004, p. 558) puts it when he addresses animation:

> It appears that current intuitive approaches to the design and use of animations can be ineffective because they do not take account of the information processing challenges posed for learners.

Two of Lowe's primary concerns about animation are that animations can 1) *overwhelm* learners by presenting complex information too fast and in a format that prohibits needed parsing and exploration, and 2) *underwhelm* learners, leaving

---

Resource

📖 Lowe, R.K. (2004). Animation and learning: Value for money? In R. Atkinson, C. McBeath, D. Jonas-Dwyer and R. Phillips (Eds), *Beyond the Comfort Zone: Proceedings of the 21st ASCILITE Conference* (pp. 558-561).

---

them to think they fully understand something they have only seen and insufficiently engaged to carry out the mental exploration and rehearsals needed to create a functioning mental model.

None of these comments are meant to overlook the great instructional assistance powerful graphics offer. Use unusual perspectives, imagery, sounds, and/or animation when it helps learners become comfortable with a contextual environment, identify concepts, focus on key information, reduce the complexity of information, witness outcomes, and so on.

But because the attention-gathering power is so great, it must be used judiciously lest it overwhelm the learner, misdirect attention, or invite analytical capabilities to doze. Be wary of any time-driven component, such as information that fades from the screen after a set delay, video,

animation, and narratives. When time-driven events are in synchronization with a learner's perception and thinking, they can keep learners intensely focused. By not having to fiddle with controls to manage them, time-driven events can serve the mind each time it's ready for another bite. That's probably why these components have such allure for some designers.

The stumbling block is that learners vary from each other in the speed they can work through a learning event. Learners even differ from day to day and moment to moment in their processing speed, whether the topic is different or the same. Their biophysical state, competing mental activity, and distractions around them are a few of the factors affecting attention and processing speed. Designers should not, therefore, assume they can match the learner's timing needs.

We certainly don't want to completely forgo, however, the power of animation and other time-driven events when they can communicate so much more expressively and effectively than other media. Consider describing appropriate movements at a complex road intersection to a beginning driver. Words are cumbersome in such a context, whereas a graphic can be extremely valuable. A bit of animation can take it to the next level or, as Lowe points out, lull the learner into a false sense of comprehension.

An effective solution is often to give learners speed and direction controls, so they can stop processes where needed, and review and play at helpful speeds. Interactivity takes them to the next step so that learners can respond to challenges, demonstrate their understanding, and practice. Such events tend to be very memorable, indeed.

Mnemonics

A mnemonic is a memory aid, such as a phrase, sentence, or poem that helps one remember something. Diagrams can also be used effectively for some content. Perhaps the most well-known example of a mnemonic is any one of the many phrases people have made up to remember the order of planets in our solar system. This one was popular when Pluto was thought to be the last of nine planets: My Very Educated Mother Just Showed Us Nine Planets (Mercury, Venus, Earth, Mars, Jupiter, Saturn, Uranus, Neptune, Pluto).

There is considerable research on the use of mnemonics to help people remember information. We have known for a long time that mnemonics work under the right conditions (Higbee, 1979). They only work, for example, if they have associations or characteristics that give them "sticking" power, such as humor, cleverness, distinctive visual image, or emotional charge. If you remember your mother as strongly promoting your education or helping you with your homework, then the example mnemonic above may have been a good one for you.

Mnemonics are particularly helpful when meaningfulness of the information to be remembered is low. The order of the planets, for example, is meaningless or "rote" information. You can only remember it through repetition or creating artificial associations, such as mnemonics. As e-learning designers, we hope that most of the content we work with can be made meaningful.

If so, we can help learners remember it by helping them create a rich network of associations. But when meaning is low, you should consider offering mnemonics and encouraging learners to invent their own.

Resources

📖 Bellezza, F.S. (1981). Mnemonic devices: Classification, characteristics, and criteria. *Review of Educational Research*, *51*(2), 247-275.

📖 Higbee, K.L. (1971). Recent research on visual mnemonics: Historical roots and educational fruits. *Review of Educational Research*, *49*(4), 611-629.

Memorable Challenge

Challenges can create memories. Meeting a challenge can make a great day. Whether it's graduating from college or using the potty successfully, we tend to remember the occasion. Of course, as with all design elements, not all challenges have equal value in learning.

Challenge difficulty, novelty, and utility contribute strongly to whether meeting a challenge will be remembered. A challenge that's far too easy, for example, even if it's the first time you've met it, is not likely to be memorable. If I challenged you to *count the number of times the letter "i" occurs in this sentence,* you could do it. But there's far too little difficulty in it for you to feel a sense of accomplishment. Further, there's little novelty and no utility, so who cares? Not you. It wouldn't be memorable. (Ok, there are 6.)

If the challenge difficulty is just right, learners may fail at first, but then succeed. Because of the failure and need to think and focus to then succeed, it's very likely these learners will remember the success and quite possibly what they did to succeed. Even if they can't remember exactly what they did, remembering a previous failure-success event gives learners confidence that they could probably figure out how to succeed again if they needed to. Allowing learners the opportunity to fail is allowing them to have one of the best and most memorable learning experiences.

Novelty can really help make events memorable, and in learning it doesn't always need to have much relevance to the way a task will actually be performed. *Ok, listen up, sales team. We're going to do some*

Memorable Challenge

Challenge Attribute	Making It Memorability
Difficulty	**Meeting a difficult challenge** tends to be remembered, but the challenge level needs to fit the individual's ability and motivation. If challenge is too low, the challenge isn't likely to be remembered. If it's too high, learners may only remember failed attempts and frustration.
Novelty	**Meeting an unusual challenge** is likely to be remembered, even if it isn't particularly difficult or valuable.
Utility	**Meeting an important challenge** or one that has been difficult to meet in the past is likely to be remembered. An authentic context can help learners assess utility.

role playing. I want each one of you to apply our sales process in conversation with the "potential clients" I'm going to bring in. Get them through each of our stages, get them to trust you, and get the information you need. You cannot use cheat sheets or any materials, and, oh yes, you can't say or write a word.

In e-learning, you can achieve novelty by letting learners do things they wouldn't ordinarily be able to do, such as run the company, travel to any location, read people's minds, experiment with dangerous chemicals, and harass coworkers. It's often helpful for learners to see issues from another perspective or play harmlessly with caustic substances or serious issues. The novelty of being able to do so can be intensely memorable.

Finally, if a challenge has utility and learners understand that utility, they are much more likely to remember the learning experience. Saving the baby pumpkins from the evil pie maker might be novel and challenging, but learners are likely just to remember the baby pumpkins and evil pie maker. HR trainees are likely to remember saving an employee from wrongful termination and, most importantly, the principles applied.

Demonstrations

Sometimes a demonstration is an excellent way to introduce a challenge. *Let me show you how it's done, and then you try it.*

There is no question that a demonstration can be helpful. Over the decade or so that I took piano lessons, I always found it helpful if my teachers would play a new piece once through for me. I quickly and easily gathered tips on tempo, expression, and technique. They shortened the learning process considerably.

Sometimes my teachers refused to give demonstrations, demanding instead that I read new pieces of music without external aids. As much as I may have complained at the time, working on my own taught me an expanded set of skills and required me to look more diligently for every marking on the score that could help.

Demonstrations are tricky things. An effective demo can give a learner at a high level of readiness almost all the direction needed to mimic and, with little practice, perform well. But demos can, and often do, dupe learners and their teachers alike. After presenting a good demo, instructors can feel they've been superbly helpful, and learners can feel as though they learned instantly and effortlessly. Later, they're both hit by the reality that none of this happened.

A good example is training on the use of software applications. After we developed Authorware, there was a demand for training classes on how to use it—especially it's advanced capabilities. Many of us had bad experiences as learners in software training, both in instructor-led classes and with e-learning, and we didn't want to go down similar paths with our learners. The biggest problems we had experienced actually centered on demonstrations.

It's very easy for learners to happily click along as a demonstration or even a "cookbook" manual directs

When are demonstrations not helpful?

Think

them. After completing a task in this way, you have seen what the application can do and you have a sense of what it takes to do it. These are good things. But in trying to repeat the steps again on your own, even immediately afterward, you often discover you can't do it at all. What one remembers about demonstrations is often limited to *I know it can be done. I saw it done. I even did it, but now...*

Because the intellect is often on hiatus during demonstrations—enjoying the ride, but striving more to keep up than to understand—little information about the decisions one has to make in performing multi-step tasks actually makes it to long-term memory. Demonstrations can be of great help to learners when confronted with a daunting challenge or when stuck in the midst of task. They belong in many learning environments, but they do not take the place of meaningful challenges. The challenge isn't usually to *see if you can follow me*; it's to solve a problem or perform a task. That is, it isn't about learning to "click" along as told; it's about knowing where and when to click.

Integration

Our ability to remember things seems to be a function of two things: the frequency with which we exercise the recall of them and the number of associations we have with them (which also tends to increase the frequency of recall). To help learners with memory, we should not only get them to practice (as we'll discuss more under Activity), but we should also help them create a rich network of associations and integrate new knowledge with existing knowledge.

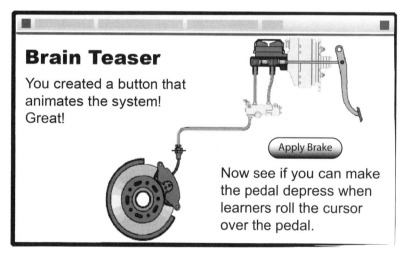

To keep learner minds active during Authorware® training and avoid click-along hypnosis, learning authors were repeatedly challenged to create interactions that were somewhat *more* advanced than a preceding demonstration created.

One excellent way of helping learners address difficult challenges, see the utility of meeting challenges, and broaden the associative networks that support their new skills is to have learners take on bigger and bigger challenges that require them to apply more of their skills. As I think again about teaching computer application skills, for example, what we found to be most successful was leading learners through a fairly simple task and then immediately challenging them to do a somewhat more difficult task on their own. That's right, we asked them to do a *more difficult task* than we had explicitly taught them to do.

Learners had to repeat components of a task they had just done in "Simon says" fashion, but this time do it on their own. Good practice. *And*, they had to modify what they did to meet the needs of a somewhat different and possibly more difficult situation. Good evaluation and adaptation. *And*, they had to recall previously learned skills and apply them. Good practice and application.

The technique required learners to think through problems, look for ways specific techniques could be generalized, and draw upon many associations to meet the challenge. This approach required them to integrate new knowledge with existing mental schema and left them with genuinely valuable skills—far more than the *click along with me* approach ever achieves. It enriched their associative network and enhanced their ability to remember.

Memorable Activity

When we talk about making learning activities memorable, it's not struggles with the e-learning application's learner interface that we want remembered. Ideally, the gestures learners use to express their thinking should be natural and easy or "transparent." Learners should need to apply very little effort and divert little attention to them.

To maximize transfer of training, we'd like activities to parallel how the behaviors will actually be performed. But unless we're teaching computer skills, there will be some level of abstraction. It's fortunate that most learners easily extrapolate interface gestures to actual behavior. Only a little imagination seems needed, even though a click of a button may represent everything from what to say in the termination of an employee to changing the altitude of a simulated plane. Some of the most complex simulations have what are essentially multiple-choice questions as their primary interface structures, and they work remarkably well to stimulate learner thinking.

Because the learner's thinking can often be naturally and easily translated into recognizable gestures, many skills can be learned via e-learning. Sometimes through good design, interface elements are far from transparent and quite instrumental in making learning events memorable. Let's look at some design decisions that can boost memory.

Switching modalities

Each type of action we can ask learners to make has attributes that will stimulate different cognitive processing. Multiple-choice ques-

tions, for example, require only the recognition of the right answer, but neither the recall of it nor the composition of it. Responses expressed through words reflect different mental processes than those expressed graphically or visually, and worded responses expressed orally differ from those expressed in written form.

It seems important to match the types of behaviors we expect learners to make in real life to the type of responses we request learners to make during training, but we know that in order to build skills we may need to start with lower levels of performance and build up. For example, we may need learners to recognize good behavior before they can actually perform it.

Many years ago, in the pioneering years of the PLATO® system, educators at the University of Illinois wanted to use e-learning to teach writing skills, but aside from the ability to check spelling and scan for the inclusion of key words and phrases, the technology to evaluate learner compositions didn't exist. What they found, however, was that learners made vast improvements in

> **Think** Are there skills that can't be taught in some part through e-learning?

their writing skills when they were given written paragraphs to evaluate and edit. The PLATO software could, in fact, judge these responses (conveyed in personal conversation with Don Bitzer, Oct. 19, 2006).

Because different modes of expression can cause learners to engage different mental models and by drawing an increased range of prior knowledge expand their associative network, it makes sense that we can maximize memorability by having learners express what they've learned through different modalities. So, here's the thought: have users respond to challenges using different modalities. Consider having them not only choose correct responses, but type their answers, write them down, draw pictures, and/or evaluate another learner's performance. The instructional objectives you have will be a guide, of course; but don't let them limit what really needs to be done.

Provide sufficient practice

While traumatic events can create indelible memories instantly, most of what we learn doesn't take root until we've practiced. Top performance requires practice, practice, practice. Perhaps it's not a new concept to revolutionize the e-learning market—a market that is continually looking for the fountain of instant authoring and chalice of effortless learning, but it's a proven concept. Practice helps us remember and perform better.

One of the best things about e-learning is that it doesn't tire out or lose patience. We can create algorithms and pools of scenarios to expeditiously let learners work as long as necessary to achieve both proficiency and lasting skills. That's why it's very peculiar that so much of e-learning fails to require sufficient practice.

While it may take a little trial and error to determine how much practice is enough, it's clear that providing just enough practice to get learners successfully through posttests is probably not enough. Unless learners will immediately begin applying new skills and practicing them often, the small gap between learning activities and real-world application may be enough to extinguish nascent abilities. And if there will be gaps of time-applications of new skills, they will likely fade unless they have been "over learned" through extensive practice or refreshed through periodic practice.

Provide spaced practice

As discussed in Chapter 7, spaced practice has much greater impact than when all practice is massed together. Rest is important for the brain and can have amazing effects. Through a process called *consolidation*, for example, learners are often able to perform even better after rest periods than they had ever performed previously.

What we might not properly intuit is how far apart spacing can be to have maximal effects. Research indicates that while spacing practice events apart by minutes actually results in beneficial effects, the benefits continue to increase with spacing of days (Thalheimer, 2006). From a pragmatic viewpoint, it's good to know that other instructional activities can occur between practice sessions. It isn't necessary to have learners blanking their minds or meditating in an incense-filled room, although there may be benefit to it.

The figure on the right illustrates an interleaving paradigm that may be optimal for many situations. Reviewing prior learning and practice intermittently sprinkled through ongoing learning events is a simple and powerful design.

It makes sense that practice sessions should be spaced further and further apart until the spacing approximates the spacing that will occur in the actual application of these skills. If, for example, a certain process is executed only on Mondays, then the spacing would ideally increase to a full week.

If use of new skills is likely to occur so infrequently that practice cannot be equally spaced, you should consider designing both performance aids and refresher learning events that can be offered just in time. While overlearning through lots of practice after learners have already reached performance competency will help sustain memory, we shouldn't expect learners to retain new skills for long periods of abstinence.

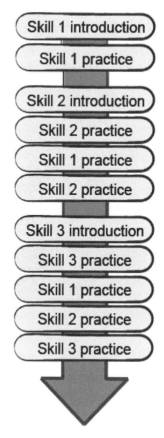

Interleaving topics provides spacing

Resource

💻 Thalheimer, W. (2006). Spacing learning events over time: What the research says. Retrieved Dec. 15, 2006, from http://www.work-learning.com/catalog/

Memorable Feedback

Television advertisers want consumers to learn positive things about their products and remember them. Similarly, we want our learners to learn useful skills and remember them. And just like so many television commercials that we remember because of humor, creativity, or outrageousness but forget what was being advertised, we fail if learners forget which actions generate which consequences. Feedback is a way of informing learners what the consequences are, and it must be memorable.

How do we create memorable ties between actions and feedback? Let me describe several successful techniques.

Intrinsic feedback

I briefly described the differences between intrinsic feedback and extrinsic feedback in the previous chapter. To refresh your memory (and to apply the principle of spacing, hopefully to your benefit!), *intrinsic feedback* focuses on the linkage between action and results—what we almost always want learn-

ers to take away—while *extrinsic feedback* focuses learners on winning approval. Let me explain.

Intrinsic feedback comes from witnessing the results of an action. A manager fails to respond to complaints of sexual harassment, and a lawsuit is filed against both the manager and the company for which she works. The lawsuit is intrinsic feedback (both in real life and in a simulated situation), and it tends to be memorable, especially if it produces emotional responses (fear, excitement, joy, etc.). It's critical, of course, that results are meaningful and matter to the learner.

Extrinsic feedback is offered by a person (or software surrogate) and usually includes judgment. *You're doing excellent work, Michael.* This kind of feedback tells learners that their job is to please the judge—the teacher or the e-learning application. While this implication is unintended (or should be) and extrinsic feedback can work learners through a course of instruction, extrinsic feedback often fails to make clear the connection between different actions and their results.

Learners come to know, *these are the good answers—the ones for which I get approval*, while, for some reason that may be entirely unclear, *these are the bad answers.* This is difficult information to remember. The difficulty comes, in part, from the realization that the instructor or e-learning application is only temporarily an authority to contend with. Just as when learners think their only evaluation will be a posttest, they fail to sufficiently rehearse for long-term retrieval. They sense their obligations to perform are temporary and short lived, and they prepare accordingly.

In addition, extrinsic feedback is difficult to remember because it's based on only a single data-point: it's correct or it's incorrect. Intrinsic feedback is much richer, showing the relationship of the action to the outcomes. *I'm being sued because an employee was humiliated. It was and is my job to ensure this doesn't happen. Although I didn't take any direct action against someone, my inaction caused damage.* This is much different from being told, *Correct answer. Inaction is a prosecutable offense.*

Vivid images

Just as with the context, strong imagery, animation, and sounds can become memorable. If they are tied to consequences of actions, they help learners remember out-comes, such as a collapsing bridge or burnt bacon. What we must always remember, however, is that these elements can be memorable on their own, and that's pretty much useless. It's the memorable commercial for, *Honey, what was that commercial for again?*

The design challenge is to reinforce the connection between specific actions and outcomes: the distinctive noise of a loose bit on an air wrench followed by the crunch of a misaligned car door not closing correctly; the image of a depressurized float on a plane making an emergency water landing; a prospective customer saying, *"Good talking to you today,"* when he's thinking, *"That guy paid no attention to the bind I'm in. I'm never buying another thing from him."*

Drama

Starting with a strong storyline in the context provides an opportunity for dramatic feedback. The drama of disastrous outcomes caused by poor performance, the amazing consequences of great performance, and even the humor outcomes from when good performance results in unintended outcomes can be memorable.

The storyline provides the connection between actions and consequences. A traveler sends a personal thank you postcard explaining how perfect the trip you set up was for his or her family. Everything went great, except that the car you rented for them was useless. It was too small for the family with all their luggage. Parking was extremely expensive in the area of the hotel you booked. And there was public transportation to all the activities on the itinerary you planned for them.

It's amazing how much detail we can recall from a story that has connected pieces. Making outcomes dramatically interesting can create a story that learners not only retell to themselves, but may also recount for others. Practice! Yes.

Memorable learning events and instructional theories

It is, of course, obvious that learning events need to be memorable, but once again, we look for broad theoretical support for making learning events memorable and techniques to do so. Bulleted below are correlating items from the mainstream design theories introduced in Chapter 5:

Cognitivism

➤ Provide active involvement of the learner in the learning process through learner control, meta-cognitive training (e.g., self-planning, monitoring, and revising techniques).

➤ Structure, organize, and sequence information to facilitate optimal processing using such cognitive strategies as outlines, summaries, synthesizers, and advance organizers.

Constructivism

➤ Principle: *actively use what is learned.* Provide learner control and the capability for learners to manipulate information.

➤ Principle: *present information in a variety of different ways.* Revisit content at different times, in rearranged contexts, for different purposes and from different conceptual perspectives.

➤ Principle: *develop pattern-recognition skills.* Support the use of problem-solving skills that allow learners to go "beyond the information given."

Minimalism

➢ Support error recognition and recovery.

➢ Exploit prior knowledge.

Merrill's First Principles of Instruction

➢ Learning is promoted when learners apply new knowledge.

➢ Learning is promoted when learners activate prior knowledge or experience.

Summary

Instructional programs need to have lasting impact. The goal is not excellent performance on a posttest; the goal is for learners to become successful performers. To achieve lasting impact, learning experiences must be memorable long after instruction has concluded.

By designing learning events that are memorable, we can support learners with the transfer of their newly acquired knowledge and skills into their everyday performance. Memorable learning events are constructed with activities, demonstrations, imagery, and storylines that offer learners opportunities to practice performance that closely resembles their on-the-job activities.

In this chapter, we again used the four components of interactive instruction—context, challenge, activity, and feedback—to itemize design decisions that can make each component contribute to the memorability of learning events. Successful design techniques for making sure learning events are memorable, and therefore able to serve the learner past the conclusion of instruction, include:

➢ Using a strong storyline, perhaps with suspense, unusual circumstances, humor, or drama that highlights the impacts of poor performance and the rewards of successful performance

➢ Employing fascinating media with unusual perspectives, imagery, sounds, and/or animation

➢ Providing imagery for concepts and/or performance consequences

➢ Providing mnemonics or having learners develop their own

➢ Demonstrating successful techniques

➢ Allowing learners to do something they wouldn't ordinarily be able to do and to undertake bigger and bigger challenges that require learners to apply more of their skills

➤ Having learners express what they've learned through different channels

➤ Providing sufficient practice that is spaced up to the point of matching the spacing that occurs on the job

➤ Using intrinsic feedback

12 | Motivational Events

[OUTSIDE WILLY WONKA'S CHOCOLATE FACTORY]

VERUCA SALT: *Daddy, I want to go in.*

MR. SALT: *It's 9:59, sweetheart.*

VERUCA SALT: *Daddy, make time go faster.*

Motivation is a wonderful thing. It focuses attention and energizes the learning process. It readies and enables people to perform.

There are many things we can't do for people, no matter how much we may wish to. We can't learn for people; they have to do it themselves. We can't develop skills for people; they have to practice themselves. We can't make people successful; they have to apply their skills. But we can help them—well, usually—and through simulation, sometimes we can even "make time go faster" so they won't lose interest.

Motivation is a prime target

Motivation is essential for learning, behavioral change, and success. With high levels of motivation, learners find a way to get information they need, obtain guidance, and practice. It's much easier to teach a highly motivated person than a moderately motivated person, and it's nigh impossible to teach completely unmotivated persons. They don't pay attention, they process little or no information, they won't practice, and nothing

Яapid readeR

- To succeed, learners must be motivated to learn and motivated to apply new skills.

- Motivation can be increased through designs that build interest and involvement.

- Motivation can be decreased by boring or irrelevant instruction.

- Video games demonstrate ways to raise motivation.

makes it into long-term memory.

Thankfully, motivation is tractable. It's a mistake to assume that the motivation learners arrive with is the greatest motivation they're going to have for learning. We can do things to heighten motivation, and unless learner motivation is already extremely high, *Show me how to work these carabiners before I lose my grip and fall off this cliff,* heightening motivation may be the single most important task for us in helping learners learn.

Success-based design

One of the reasons successful e-learning designers are constantly looking for ways to avoid boring learners is that boring events diminish motivation. With diminished motivation, all the hard work invested in the design and development of learning events will come to naught. On the other hand, interesting events feed and strengthen motivation, making both instruction and learning easier and easier. With heightened motivation, learners take maximum advantage of the learning aids provided, and everyone succeeds.

Seven magic keys

Over the years, from looking at hundreds of e-learning applications, I've identified seven highly effective ways to increase and maintain heightened learner motivation. I don't doubt that there are other effective techniques as well, but I do know that this set is unusually powerful. If you employ just a couple of them in each project you design, you'll most certainly have more successful e-learning than most. If you get three or more of them incorporated, I think you'll be amazed.

The *Seven Magic Keys* to motivating e-learners, listed within the framework of the four components of interactivity design are:

Context

1. Build anticipation of outcomes.
2. Make the context appealing (use novelty, suspense, humor, fascinating graphics, sound, music, animation, etc.).

Challenge

3. Put the learner at risk.
4. Select the right content for each learner
   - If previously learned, repetition will be boring
   - Adjust the challenge level to match the learner's readiness level
   - Provide challenges that integrate previous learning and provide spaced practice
   - Provide challenges that build confidence

Activity

5. Have the learner perform multi-step tasks.

Feedback

6. Provide intrinsic feedback.
7. Delay judgment.

Learning from games

Successful video games demonstrate that motivation can be sustained over long periods of time. Examining their techniques as Gee (2003) has done provides considerable direction for e-learning, especially with regard to motivation and practice. Some of the 38 principles of learning he deduced from his analysis are directly on target with what works in e-learning design and are included below within the discussions of motivating contexts, challenges, activities, and feedback.

Motivational Context

The first few moments of a book, an opera, a movie, a play, or a video game are particularly important. They either capture the audience's attention and interest in what may happen next, or they lose it. If you lose it at the beginning, where the creator is expected to do some of his best work, it's hard to convince the audience that they should stay alert throughout. And if you've lost their attention, you'll have to work doubly hard to regain it.

GEE PRINCIPLE 23
Subset Principle

Learning even at its start takes place in a (simplified) subset of the real domain.

Resource

Gee, J.P. (2003). *What Video Games Have to Teach Us About Learning and Literacy.* New York: Palgrave Macmillan.

Committed Learning Principle

Learners participate in an extended engagement (lots of effort and practice) as extensions of their real-world identities in relation to a virtual identity to which they feel some commitment and a virtual world that they find compelling.

Build outcome anticipation

In general, people love to guess what's going to happen. Some readers I know like to read the last chapter of a novel first to decide if they think the book is worth reading. We're clearly not all alike. But although I think reading the last chapter diminishes the reading experience a book will be able to provide, the willingness some people have to sacrifice a bit of a book's punch, maybe even the biggest plot twist, in order to know what the story leads to, makes an important point: we hate to waste our time.

e-Learners hate to waste their time. They want to be convinced, as soon as possible, that a learning program is going to provide a worthwhile experience. Now, what constitutes a worthwhile experience is definitely arguable and individual, but in my experience, most learners first want the experience to be enjoyable—to feel good, be fun, keep them interested, and secondarily to enable specific skills.

This may be because so much e-learning has been painful and provided minimal benefits. Learners want to know first that they aren't going to be tortured. If an application begins well, learners are probably willing to delay judgment on the skills-related value for a bit, and hope that the experience will, in fact, be beneficial. Once again, we can see why starting with a dreary list of objectives is not the smartest thing to do. Presenting lengthy instructions on how to work the application's controls isn't any better.

What is smart is getting learners into something fascinating right away and setting their expectations for personally valuable outcomes. It could be a demonstration of something amazing and unexpected that the tool to be learned can do. It could be a statement such as, *In twenty minutes here, you will have learned to do something that at least 300 million people in this country wish they could do. Or, Hate making cold calls. You're going to learn how to kill the pain and make them fun.*

Of course, actually getting into it and delivering observable improvement of useful skills quickly is the best way of building motivational anticipation. To do this, it helps if the contextual situation 1) is understandable, of course, 2) is somewhat complex, and 3) can be broken down into sub-challenges that the learner can reasonably tackle.

GEE PRINCIPLE 1

Active, Critical Learning Principle

All aspects of the learning environment...are set up to encourage active and critical, not passive, learning.

Complex situations are likely to be interesting. Indeed, we know people are drawn to complexity even from childhood (Willis and Dornbush, 1968). It's the way we're wired. Complexity generates curiosity, and that's something we definitely want in our learners.

In contrast, consider an overly simple situation: *These meal tickets were added incorrectly* and a situation that makes no sense to learners: *The new DCC shuts the entire system down when previously undetectable short*

Resource

📖 Willis, E.J. and Dornbush, R.L. (1968). Preference for visual complexity. *Child Development, 39*(2) 639-646.

circuits occur at turnouts and trip the district booster. You probably aren't excited about jumping in to resolve either of these situations.

A challenge, perhaps the only clear challenge, arising from the first situation is: *See if you can add the meal tickets correctly.* Boring. Even if the objective were simply to develop the ability to add monetary values, it's hardly motivational.

More interesting would be this situation: *In some months, Harry found his restaurant earned what he expected to make, but in other months of serving the same meals and number of diners, he lost so much, he had to let staff go.* Challenges emanate nicely from this situation, including one or more for the addition objective. For example: *See if you can find Harry's problem. Here are twenty typical meal checks from each month, together with what his customers paid and his costs based on meals served.*

With this approach, waiters would practice double-checking the math on meal tickets—the context in which the skills are actually performed—and also see how important getting the correct totals is. Without the power of an interesting and appropriate set of context and challenges, your waiters would probably amaze you with excuses to avoid practice.

When a situation makes no sense to learners, such as the one with the DCC system (which would make no sense to you at all unless you're using advanced electronics on a model railroad), you're more likely to generate learner frustration and anxiety than interest. The solution, however, isn't to substitute simplified understandable situations that no one cares about. The solution is to express the situation in terms learners can understand and appreciate, and then devise a series of challenges to bring learner ability up to the point of doing something that's understandably valuable.

For example, instead of: *The new DCC shuts the entire system down when previously undetectable short circuits occur at turnouts and trip the district booster*, you might convey the situation in these terms: *Some of our customers are having problems with their model trains when they convert to the popular new digital "command" control systems we carry.* A challenge that builds outcome interest might then be: *As a customer service representative, determine whether the control system is defective when customers report that their system shuts down unexpectedly.*

Because the ultimate performance target is presented initially, it will be easier to interest learners in pursuing the enabling objectives with lower-level challenges. Objectives related to such things as differentiating between digital systems and non-digital (analog) systems, describing a short circuit, and listing common causes of short circuits now make sense and have a purpose. There's a reason to pursue them beyond someone asking you to do it.

Appealing contexts

e-Learning applications are often skinned with beautiful graphics. With the beauty so frequently only skin deep, however, disappointment comes quickly as a few interactions reveal what's underneath. So, it's with some trepidation that I point out that appealing contexts can entice learners who are somewhat lacking in motivation. Once into the application, great interactions can take it from there.

Appeal can be achieved in a variety of ways. A great graphic look is a terrific asset, and with the power-

> **Think**
>
> Identify a few tasks that require considerable practice to learn. Then think of contexts that would make learners enjoy practicing.

ful tools available today to create them, why not? But why not also use the appeal of a fascinating story, suspense, humor, sounds, music, and novelty? A little creativity can produce greater power than a cool look.

One very effective e-learning application that teaches management skills and decision making starts out with these words, center screen: *Olivia's husband has just passed away from cancer. She's requesting your approval for three weeks off from work.*

It really doesn't matter much what the screen graphics are at this point. Learners are instantly drawn in.

Motivational Challenge

Challenges are almost inherently motivational, especially if they are well matched to the learner. Neither challenges that are too difficult nor challenges that are too easy have the motivation of a challenge that's just right—doable but with risk involved.

Risk

Let's look at risk first.

When are we most alert? When we sense that we're at risk. When are we least alert? When we feel safe,

relaxed, and comfortable enough to sleep; in other words, when there's no perceptible risk.

GEE PRINCIPLE 6
"Psychosocial Moratorium" Principle

Learners can take risks in a space where real-world consequences are lowered.

GEE PRINCIPLE 28
Discovery Principle

Overt telling is kept to a well-thought-out minimum, allowing ample opportunity for the learner to experiment and make discoveries.

The Motivational Power of Challenges
"I triple-dog dare you."
From the movie, *A Christmas Story* (MGM, 1983).

We want learners to be alert; not panicked, obviously, but alert enough to be actively and carefully surveying the circumstances and considering options. Some example challenges that might do this are:

➤ *Using the data provided, complete the insurance application form within 8 minutes. If you do not finish in time or you make any errors, you will have to start over.*

➤ *Analyze each bank check as it appears on the screen to be sure all necessary components are present. For each check you incorrectly accept or reject, six more checks will be added to the exercise.*

➤ *You typed 27 words per minute on your first attempt. This was very good, as the average of all learners is 24 words per minute on the first attempt. Let's see if you can now get at least 30.*

The privacy afforded by e-learning makes it possible to use risk as a motivator without chancing public embarrassment or humiliation. It can be quite effective to let learners see that poor performance will be called out frankly, especially, of course, when encouragement and praise for meaningful accomplishments are also given. Citing the performance of others can help too, especially in the privacy of e-learning where learners lack a sense of how their performance stacks up against others. It seems most people really want to know.

Since learners can freeze up when risk pushes anxiety too high, designers use risk as a motivator most successfully when providing safety valves to prevent overdoing it. Here are some techniques:

➤ Allowing learners to set and vary the level of challenge

➤ Providing hints and even the correct answers when learners are stuck

➤ Complimenting learners on their efforts, even when they fail

➤ Interleaving easier challenges (spaced practice!) to remind learners of their advancing skills

Selecting the right content for each learner

Given a context that is fitting for both the content and targeted population of learners, it's up to the challenges to define and initiate the learning experiences. And the challenges need to be right for each learner if we are to maintain positive motivation. By selecting specific content and setting the level for each interactive event, challenges provide a critical means of individualization and invigorating learner motivation.

e-Learning applications have particular value and an advantage over most other instructional interventions, because they can easily select and even modify parameters of learning challenges in real time. Although complex algorithms for matching instructional treatments to preferred learning styles have been explored for years, it appears the biggest payoffs come less in fine tuning and more in the broader stokes of

selecting content, sequencing activities, and giving adult learners the control they need to feel in control.

Some rules for effective selection of content are:

> Adjust the challenge level to match the learner's readiness level.

> If previously learned, don't try to teach it again. Instructional redundancy is boring: *I know, I know, you've already said that.* (Practice is something different, although it can certainly be boring as well.)

> Provide challenges that integrate previous learning.

> Provide spaced practice.

> Provide challenges that build confidence.

GEE PRINCIPLE 24
Incremental Principle
Learning situations are ordered in the early stages so that earlier cases lead to generalizations that are fruitful for later cases.

GEE PRINCIPLE 14
"Regime of Competence" Principle
The learner gets ample opportunity to operate within, but at the outer edge of his or her resources so that, at those points, things are felt as challenging but not undoable.

GEE PRINCIPLE 13
Ongoing Learning Principle
The distinction between learner and master is vague, since learners... must, at higher and higher levels, undo their routinized mastery to adapt to new or changed conditions. There are cycles of new learning, automatization, undoing automatization, and new, reorganized automatization.

As Dirksen (2006) points out, most e-learning applications work in a fairly linear fashion from simple to difficult challenges. Each subsequent challenge heaps on new content in an ever-forward moving direction. This is very much in contrast to the design of motivating video games, which take time to let learners revel in their newly acquired skills, gain confidence, and then move on.

In short, many e-learning designs get learners involved in far too little practice, lump practice exercises

Resource

Dirksen, J. (2006, December). *BAM! EEEEEK! POW! What video games can teach us about e-learning feedback.* Paper presented at the e-Learning Guild Online Forum on Designing and Developing Online Assessments and Evaluations.

Typical designs string modules of instruction together, adding content and increasing challenge difficulty throughout.

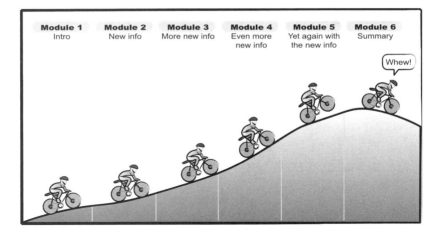

Game designers know that keeping interest high is paramount to successful design. They mix, often masterfully, new content with review and practice of previous skills, with varying levels of challenge.

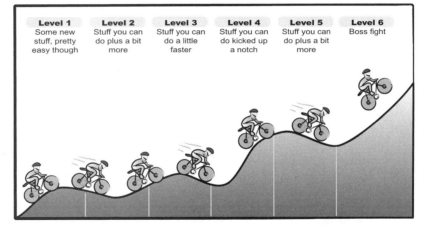

In contrast, typical e-learning designs exhaust learners.

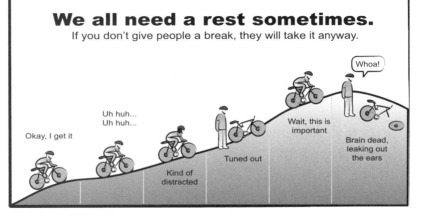

together into one or a very few sessions, spend too little time letting new mental frameworks take root, deprive learners of opportunities to enjoy the fruits of their learning efforts, and exhaust learners in the process.

Motivational Activity
Multi-step tasks

Through the ingenuity of interface designers, it's become possible to express a lot of what we're thinking and request what we want through a single click. Unfortunately, the real world isn't that kind and rarely has things so carefully and neatly organized for our command. We usually have to do a fair amount of information gathering before we can do the organizing so we can finally make decisions and carry out important tasks.

If we want learners to find their learning tasks both interesting and authentic enough to have applicability, activities should include more realistic tasks than: *Click here.* Most real-world activities are multi-step tasks and provide multiple oppor-

tunities for error. Of course, they also provide multiple opportunities for us to correct our errors. Good e-learning designs should do likewise.

GEE PRINCIPLE 16
Multiple Routes Principle
There are multiple ways to make progress or move ahead. This allows learners to make choices, rely on their own strengths and styles of learning and problem solving, while also exploring alternative styles.

Focus aids

That's not to say that we're not there to assist learners. Advantages we have over on-the-job learning are that we can speed things up, so learners have opportunities for many more practice exercises than they would otherwise have. We can have some steps completed or done automatically, so learners can focus on isolated aspects of a process. We can reduce safety hazards, so mistakes are beneficial rather than harmful.

Just as the television chef can put a pot roast in the oven and instantly pull it out, steaming hot and savory, we can provide a little magic of our own to complete tasks instantly—even tasks the learner has no comprehension of. One of the motivating principles Gee found in video games is just this:

GEE PRINCIPLE 10
Amplification of Input Principle
For a little input, learners get a lot of output.

The magic is not lost on learners. They enjoy feeling powerful and being able to get a lot done quickly. And the ability to focus or restrict the decision arena gives learners a chance to build confidence before dealing with an overwhelming number of options. Getting a balance between authentic multi-step interactions and keeping the learning space focused is important, but not always difficult. Don't forget that adult learners like control. Allowing them to determine when they want help to be available and when they feel like going it alone or taking on a greater scope of responsibility is almost always effective.

Motivational Feedback
Intrinsic feedback
Once again, the practice of preferring intrinsic feedback to extrinsic feedback is relevant. Motivational

Motivational Feedback

games exceed in applying the Achievement Principle:

GEE PRINCIPLE 11
Achievement Principle
For learners of all levels of skill there are intrinsic rewards from the beginning, customized to each learner's level, effort, and growing mastery and signaling the learner's ongoing achievements.

We've covered the concept and means of providing intrinsic feedback well enough elsewhere, but the fact that it comes up as useful not only for motivation, but also for meaningfulness and memorability suggests that intrinsic feedback is extremely important. And noting that so much e-learning has none suggests that it is an area on which designers need to forget whatever is driving them to extrinsic feedback and do something far more interesting.

Delayed judgment
One of the advantages that people often list is that e-learning can immediately score answers. Indeed, it is a capability that contrasts with what human instructors can do. When I was in school, we used to think an instructor was unusually dedicated if we got graded papers

back the day after we handed them in. But that's painfully slow compared to what e-learning can do.

Being able to immediately evaluate answers doesn't mean, however, that it's always a good thing to let learners know whether their responses were good, poor, or somewhere between. Intrinsic feedback can be given without judgment and often should. *Now that you've added the egg yolks to the dry ingredients, you have a very thick sticky dough. Is thick sticky dough good or bad?* We've not said, and the learner needs to think about it. That's intrinsic feedback without judgment. So is: *Your employee is upset that you've told him, "I can't talk with you about it now, in the hallway, fifteen minutes before a big meeting, even though you feel you have a matter of great personal concern to discuss. We'll have to talk afterward."*

At some point, as learners develop skills, it's important for them to assess the appropriateness of their intermediate actions. Relying on immediate judgment is an artificial crutch that won't be present in real-world performance, and not having it present in some learning events both allows more authentic practice and makes the process more

interesting. *The dough hasn't been sticky before; I must not have added all the dry ingredients I need. – It's important that I have the ability to listen carefully and fully in a private setting when employees have concerns. Although delays are regrettable, sometimes they are necessary, even if it's unsettling to employees.*

GEE PRINCIPLE 15
Probing Principle
For learners of all levels of skill, there are intrinsic rewards from the beginning, customized to each learner's level, effort, and growing mastery and signaling the learner's ongoing achievements.

Delaying judgment puts more onus on learners to evaluate intrinsic feedback and determine if they are on a proper course. If they need to deal with unfortunate consequences of an error, as is often the case, it's important that they learn and practice these skills as with all others.

In contrast, if judgment is immediate, learners often take to submitting any answer, even a wild flurry of guesses, just to see what the feedback will be. When you yield the correct answer, they'll say to themselves: *Oh, yeah. I know that,* even when they don't. Through such a strategy, learners make no commitment to

---

Tip: You might not have considered the need for learners to evaluate the results of their own actions when you first prepared learning objectives. Perhaps one or more objectives should be added to address this important skill.

---

their answers, focus more on judgment than the consequences of their answers, and learn at a very shallow level.

Interestingly, and perhaps counter-intuitively, we've found in our practice that if you give learners an explicit option to ask for the correct answer, as opposed to automatically getting it in response to a submitted answer, learners are quite hesitant to ask. Many, although not all, will try very hard to determine the correct path before giving up. This process can be enhanced by placing a limit on the number of times they can ask for the answer, say three for an often-workable number. In this case, learners will typically do all they can to keep their three safety nets intact for as long as possible, just as they do on TV game shows.

On the other hand, there's no advantage in developing a habit of submitting wild guesses. Wild guessing won't be a problem if challenges are of appropriate difficulty. Referring back to Gee's Principle 14, we want learners operating at

the "outer edge" of their resources, but sufficiently within bounds that challenges are "not undoable."

Adult learners are uncomfortable when no supporting resources are at hand, so it's wise to provide access.

GEE PRINCIPLE 27
Explicit Information On-Demand and Just-in-Time Principle
The learner is given explicit information both on-demand and just-in-time, when the learner needs it or just at the point where the information can best be understood and used in practice.

The combination of multi-step tasks, intrinsic feedback, and delayed judgment is powerful and the mainstay of the success-based designer when tasks involving decision-points and alternative behaviors are being taught.

Prescriptive outcomes

Finally, there's another important type of feedback. It's neither intrinsic nor extrinsic, actually, but simply an adjustment of subsequent events. Depending on how well the learner is performing, he or she may be jumped ahead to more complex challenges or dropped back to remedial exercises.

Corrective Feedback Paradigm

An excellent example of prescriptive outcomes that helps learners practice effectively is the Corrective Feedback Paradigm (CFP) based on research by Siegel and Misselt (1984). Simply stated, when there is a set of independent problems to solve, problems are presented to the learner one at a time. Although values of the paradigm can be varied, let's say the learner must correctly solve each problem correctly three times in a row before we will consider the learner to have mastered it.

Let's examine the paradigm by first following what happens when the learner responds correctly. Then we'll take up what happens when the learner fails to solve a problem.

The learner is given a problem and solves it correctly for the first time. The problem is reinserted into the problem queue so that it will come up again about six problems later. When it is reencountered, the learner once again responds correctly, and now the problem is once again reinserted in the queue, possibly at the end, or if there are sufficient problems in the queue, ten or more problems back. If, when it is reencountered for the third time, the learner once again demonstrates proficiency, the problem is retired for good.

Resource

Siegel, M. and Misselt, A.L. (1984). Adaptive feedback and review paradigm for computer-based drills. *Journal of Educational Psychology, 76*(2) 310-317.

Now, what happens when the learner responds inadequately? Once again, the problem is reinserted in the queue but a bit closer to the top so that the learner will encounter it soon. We'll put it in the third position, so that the learner will take on two other problems before trying this one again. It's important, of course, that we have given the learner instruction so that there is reason to think he or she will be able to respond correctly on the next try, given that the learner can remember long enough.

And this is actually the point of the paradigm. Whether you explain the process or not, learners quickly deduce how the paradigm works and anticipate reencountering failed problems. In our case, they will expect to see the failed problem after attempting to solve two others. They will do their best to rehearse the

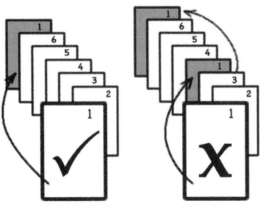

Correctly solved problems are worked again later to ensure mastery

Failed problems are reworked at increasing intervals of delay.

problem and solution in their minds so that they will succeed on the second try. Otherwise, of course, the problem continues to be reinserted in the queue, over and over again.

At the point when a learner correctly solves a problem, that problem switches over to the process of handling correct responses. After three correct responses in a row, the problem retires. If, however, an incorrect response is given at any point, that problem is restarted in the sequence established for all incorrect answers.

While there are many other ways of branching instruction and content based on learner performance, this paradigm has been thoroughly researched and, perhaps more importantly, used successfully in many e-learning applications. It is highly recommended.

Motivational learning events and instructional theories

Ironically, motivation has been something of a sleeper among issues taken on by instructional designers, but theorists have long recognized the need for learning motivation.

Bulleted below for cross-reference are principles and techniques cited in the theories introduced in Chapter 5 that address learning motivation:

Cognitivism

➤ Emphasis on the active involvement of the learner in the learning process [learner control, meta-cognitive training (e.g., self-planning, monitoring, and revising techniques)]

➤ Creation of learning environments that allow and encourage students to make connections with previously learned material [recall of prerequisite skills; use of relevant examples, analogies]

Constructivism

➤ The need for information to be presented in a variety of different ways [revisiting content at different times, in rearranged contexts, for different purposes, and from different conceptual perspectives]

➤ Supporting the use of problem-solving skills that allow learners to go "beyond the information given" [developing pattern-recognition skills, presenting alternative ways of representing problems]

➤ Assessment focused on transfer of knowledge and skills [presenting new problems and situations that differ from the conditions of the initial instruction]

Minimalism

➤ Getting started fast

➤ Coordinating system and training

➤ Developing optimal training designs

Merrill's First Principles

➤ Integration principle: learning is promoted when learners integrate their new knowledge into their everyday world.

Summary

Creating motivating learning experiences for learners seems to be an obvious objective of any instructional development effort. However, creation of motivating designs is taking it's time finding its way into mainstream e-learning development practice.

Throughout this chapter I have discussed how motivation is essential for learning, behavioral change, and success, and how a motivated learner will find a way to get needed information, obtain guidance, and engage in practice, whereas an unmotivated learner is sure to fail.

The *Seven Magic Keys* provide direction for designing motivating e-learning. They were reviewed within the framework of the four components of interactivity design:

Context

1. Build anticipation of outcomes
2. Make the context appealing

Challenge

3. Put the learner at risk
4. Select the right content for each learner

Activity

5. Have the learner perform multi-step tasks

Feedback

6. Provide intrinsic feedback
7. Delay judgment

Instruction

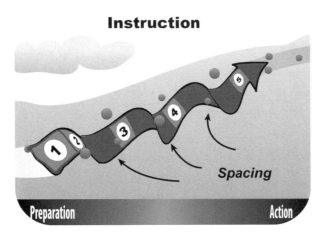

Designers of interactive video games have demonstrated how engaging and motivating software applications can be. In this regard, game designers have been far more successful than e-learning designers, and we have much to learn from their work.

In this chapter, helpful principles of design identified from the analysis of video games by James Gee (2003) are interleaved with approaches for building motivational contexts, challenges, activities, and feedback.

As reflected here (left) in the diagram of the learning process we have been constructing throughout this book, an important technique of game designers is to alternate increased levels of challenge with opportunities to practice and enjoy the application of new skills. A steady increase in challenge, as is typical of many e-learning designs, is exhausting. It often precludes the amount of practice that is necessary for learners to secure their new abilities and gain confidence. But by both steadily increasing the spacing of learning events and periodically raising and easing the challenge level, we can keep learners engaged in practice and building skills that will be resistant to extinction.

13 | Designing Performance Aids

Tony was an extraordinary high school basketball coach. He knew technique and how to teach it. He knew how to communicate with his players. Perhaps most importantly, he knew how to motivate his players to do their best.

Tony was a demanding coach, requiring much more practice and double the fitness training previous coaches had required.

The day before the first game of the season, however, Tony saluted his team, thanked them for their hard work, and wished them luck. The team was trained, he had done his job, and Tony had booked a vacation.

Tony was fired.

It's all about performance

It's the goal, the reason, the justification for instructional design. Performance. The proof pudding.

It's a simple concept, *doing the right thing at the right time*, but not so easy to accomplish. It requires more than meets the eye, such as:

➤ Knowing what the "right" response is to specific situations

➤ Recognizing when "the time" is right

➤ Being able to do the right thing

➤ And finally, actually doing it—properly performing the right action at the right time

Also implied, but important not to overlook, is the need to differentiate between situations that require modification of a usual response, substitution of another response altogether, or deliberately and appropriately deciding not to respond in favor of doing other things.

There are many opportunities to fail and yet only one way to succeed, and that one way actually, consistently performing effectively. As Cervantes put it in *Don Quixote de La Mancha,* "the proof is in the pudding." It's not the talent of the cook, the effort, the vision or

Яapid readeR

- Success results not from high posttest scores but from effective behavior.

- Nascent skills are easily lost if not applied and practiced.

- Providing rewards, countering excuses, controlling the environment, and creating helpful relationships can help transfer learning to performance.

intention. The true value of culinary talent and most everything can be judged only when it is put to use. If the pudding is lumpy, sour, or displeasing in any way, the performance was insufficient. Similarly, if our learners fail to act and act effectively, whether it's caused by lack of sensing the proper situations, lack of confidence, lack of ability, or anything else, we've failed to reach the goal.

Even with well-developed skills, many factors can inhibit the transfer of training to proper performance. Fortunately, designers can improve chances of successful outcomes by anticipating and countering adverse forces. Not providing support for transfer of training into applied proficient behaviors is commonplace, however, and such lack of intervention unfortunately accounts for the lack of success many learning programs suffer.

In this chapter, we look at a point where the learning process typically breaks down, undermines all that has been accomplished, and fails to achieve the performance goal. It's that period after learning, when learners may not have an immediate opportunity to apply their new capabilities or where they encounter somewhat unexpected conditions that things break down. Here again, learning practice and research agree with behavioral change research: the probability of success is much greater if learners are given support rather than left simply to fend for themselves.

Rather than calling it quits at the end of the Instruction Phase, organizations need to design and develop aids to help learners transfer their learning to performance. Techniques covered in this chapter are:

> Training supervisors to mentor
> Basing evaluation on observed performance
> Encouraging self-testing
> Teaching safety nets
> Providing refresher events and spaced practice
> Applying behavioral change techniques of reward, countering, controlling the environment, and helping relationships

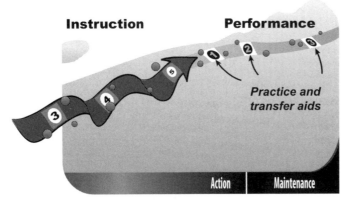

Training supervisors

Supervisors of recent learners are in a position to help make sure learners continue to practice new skills, improve performance, and receive helpful feedback, but they are hindered in their ability to do so unless they are privy to what learners have been learning to do. It seems obvious, of course, but I've witnessed situations in which organizations, in a rush to introduce new services to their customers, began by putting only their front-line employees through training. They bypassed supervisors, except to direct them to get their people into training as soon as possible.

The supervisors couldn't give guidance, and feared looking inept in the eyes of their subordinates. Also feeling a bit alienated, the supervisors quite actively, although discreetly, dissuaded their teams from implementing the new practices after they had completed the training. This is not a success scenario.

To maximize the effectiveness of learning programs, it's always wise to consider first educating supervisors and other people who will directly influence what learners do following instruction. It isn't always necessary for supervisors to be highly proficient performers themselves, even to serve as a bit of a mentor. But it is necessary for those in a position to give guidance to know what behaviors are appropriate under specific conditions. And they need to know how to mentor.

Mentoring

In a study of mentoring offered subsequent to classroom training, Bane et al. (1997) found that while the training program increased productivity by 28 percent, the addition of mentoring increased productivity to 88 percent! Quite often, however, the activities of training programs are confined to learning activities, between the pre-instructional and performance phases, where they can't help learners ready themselves for learning and change, and where they can't offer the real-time guidance learners need in the application of new skills. But with the magnitude of impact post-training support can provide, successful designers do all they can to insist on the provision of mentoring and/or other support.

Resource

   📖 Bane, D., Kopelman, R.E., and Olivero, G. (1997). Executive coaching as a transfer of training tool: Effects on productivity in a public agency. *Public Personnel Management, 26,* 461-469.

Consider providing performance aids for supervisors in the form of checklists about good performance based on what learners are being taught. Provide examples of poor performance in addition to the hallmarks of good performance to give supervisors the most help. A list of frequently asked questions and answers might also be helpful.

Consider providing a calendar of activities for supervisors that suggests periodic checking in with learners to observe their performance, ask if they have any questions or concerns, and provide reminders and tips.

Make sure that supervisors are aware that new skills will fade unless learners practice. You might suggest careful assignment of tasks, perhaps with rotating assignments to give learners the practice they need in situations where some types of tasks occur infrequently.

Basing evaluation on observed performance

Forget posttests. Why do you use them? To measure the effectiveness of the instruction? To differentiate performers from each other? To certify people? To provide grades or measures of learning? To motivate learners to study?

Forget It!

None of these are good reasons for posttests, because posttest measure something very peculiar and of little value. Unless we're actually preparing people to take a certification test (which is another practice we could easily chastise), tests measure more test-taking and short-term abilities than competence. As we've discussed, learners are strategic in the use of their mental resources and the expenditure of effort. If they think the primary use of their learning is going to be the achievement of a good posttest score, they will study in such a way that there will be little residual capability after the posttest has been taken. The *posttest paradox* is that, while a posttest may encourage learners to study, it also prepares them to forget.

We can better motivate learners and also assess everything from the effectiveness of instructional programs to the relative competencies of learners if we measure their actual performance in the conditions we have targeted. To achieve effective motivation, tell learners, *Your learning will be evaluated by observing your actual performance ("on the job," if appropriate) about six weeks following the conclusion of this course.* Learners will prepare themselves differently and in more useful ways.

Encouraging self-testing

Although we often look to others to give us feedback about the adequacy of our performance, people who are motivated to change their behaviors and succeed will appreciate help with checking their own performance. You can provide forms, electronic or paper, that list criteria for performance excellence. Learners will be reminded of key performance principles as they score themselves. You might also consider having recent learners forward their own rating sheets to supervisors. Implementing such a process lets learners know that progress is important and that we trust their own assessments. Reporting progress can give learners a way of rewarding themselves, just as it gives supervisors an opportunity to provide recognition and encouragement.

Teaching safety nets

It's much easier to stalemate an undesired behavior by substituting a preferred one than it is to simply extinguish a bad habit or reflex. Imagine practicing the habit of blowing out a match or lighter every time there's a flame in your face. Although persons trying to quit smoking would have already made a few bad decisions if they had a cigarette between their lips, there's a chance that if they had practiced blowing out a flame before they could light a cigarette, they might actually catch themselves, blow out the match, and throw the cigarette away.

> **Think**
> We often simplify to help learners grasp concepts, but what should we do to help learners deal with the complex realities that challenge behavioral change?

When performing new behaviors, there will be mistakes and setbacks. Instructional activities at this point in the process should be devised to help learners anticipate setbacks and teach them what to do when they've taken a few bad turns. Without an honest recognition of the probability of error, and with no rehearsed plan for dealing with setbacks, learners may easily give up completely at the first failure, returning to more familiar and comfortable behaviors.

Providing refresher events and practice

As we discussed earlier, don't forget that one of the most powerful influences we can wield is spaced practice. Even during periods subsequent to instruction in which learners are expected to perform, it can be very helpful to provide refresher learning events to counter forgetting and degradation of performance quality than often happens over time in response to the barrage of behavioral influences we face. Gradually

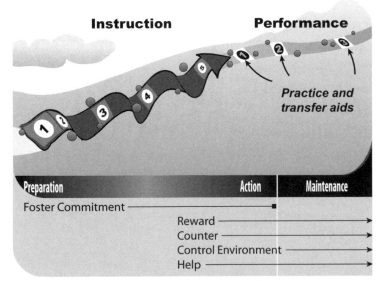

Performance Change Aids

increasing the spacing between practice sessions helps fight the decline of performance ability.

Applying behavioral change techniques

New behaviors finally emerge in the fourth stage (Action) and become routine in the fifth stage, (Maintenance) of the Prochaska Stages of Change model. At first, nascent behaviors are weak and in uneasy competition either with previous behaviors or no pattern of response at all. Social Liberation and Fostering Commitment, which were helpful in earlier stages, continue as appropriate ways to help learners acquire new behaviors. With both the support of the people around them and a steady commitment, learners have a much better prospect of reaching performance goals.

In these later stages, four techniques can be applied: rewarding, countering, controlling the environment, and helping learners by building strong, trusting relationships.

Rewarding

Behaviorism, with its stimulus and reward constructs, is quite out of favor due to its oversimplification of what determines human behavior and lack of effectiveness to achieve long-term behavioral changes (Rock and Schwartz, 2006), and yet, reward does have an important positive effect when it is used to keep learners focused on solutions (rather than problems). In studying the neuroscience of leadership, Rock and Schwartz argue that positive feedback offered as "… a deliberate effort to reinforce behavior that already works, which, when conducted skillfully, is one aspect of behaviorism that has beneficial cognitive effect. In a brain that is also constantly pruning connections while making new ones, positive feedback may play a key functional role as 'a signal to do more of something'" (p. 6).

Resource

🖳 Rock, D. and Schwartz, J. The neuroscience of leadership. Downloaded on Oct. 16, 2006 from www.strategy-business.com/press/freearticle/06207?tid=230&pg=all

The key concept here is actually *attention density*, or the amount of attention focused over a defined period of time. Attention to behavioral change activates mental maps, sets expectations, and helps learners succeed in their first forays. It is perhaps the primal cognitive activity needed to effect behavioral change.

So why is attention density mentioned here in the context of reward? The reason rewards may actually work in the complex area of behavioral change is not so much because they provide incentives, but rather because they help learners focus, pay attention, and keep desired performance attributes in mind. Effective rewards are likely to be those that heighten attention density and may be offered simply in the form of feedback that identifies points of success or progress or recognition of continuing effort and commitment.

Countering

Since it's easier to replace behaviors than it is to extinguish them, the most successful technique to stop excessive eating or worrying is often the introduction of new incompatible behaviors, beginning with the substitution of different thoughts for those that lead to undesirable behaviors. *Countering* is just such a technique to prohibit thinking negatively and focus attention on undesirable behaviors by stimulating positive thoughts and initiating behaviors that are incompatible with bad behaviors.

Sociologists and psychologists report considerable success with countering behaviors, suggesting, for example, that when between meal hunger strikes, be ready to go do something you really enjoy, whether it's petting your cat, playing the piano, or going for a walk.

In corporate and educational settings, we're less often dealing with the discontinuance of behaviors than with the upgrading or addition of new ones, but we are still contending with laziness, inaction, or tendencies to cut corners—all behavioral options that learners may find attractive. Countering plans can be just as effective, if not more effective, since alternative behaviors may not be as strongly competitive in general education and training applications.

Controlling the environment

There are many cues in our environment that influence our behavior. As I'm writing this chapter, I'm sitting in my home office, because when I'm at my work office I have many distractions that prevent prolonged focus. It's not always interruptions, although they are problematic. If I hit a writer's block, in that environment, for example, it's very easy for me to pick up another task or enter into a conversation that consumes the rest of the day.

Here at home, however, I still need to control the environment so that I can be optimally productive. My office is not far away from the refrigerator, the cookie jar, and the remains of our holiday desserts. It's easy to get up to "stretch my legs," arriving without intention in the kitchen for a little comfort food. Realizing this was happening far too often, I've changed things around so that I have a cup warmer to keep my tea hot and healthy snacks nearby. When I get up to stretch my legs, I actually do that. I walk away from the kitchen (no need to go there now) and even go outside for a brisk walk when the weather permits.

Almost everyone can make a change in his or her environment to assist performance improvement. Cashiers are often told to tell departing customers, "Have a great day." But I saw a personally scribbled note posted on a cash register recently that said, "Be the bright spot in everybody's day." That cashier managed to say something cheerful and encouraging to everybody she rang through.

You can help learners:

➤ Identify and avoid situations that are associated with poor performance, perhaps by rescheduling their daily routine

➤ Reframe how they see and therefore react to situations, perhaps by seeing an upset customer's complaint as an opportunity to create a grateful and loyal customer

➤ Reconstruct situations, perhaps by moving furniture, equipment, forms, or other supplies

➤ Create and use checklists, reminders, and other performance aids, perhaps by having customizable examples online

Building Helpful relationships

So many things in life are easier with a little help from our friends. In the work environment, where there is often so much stress and competition, it can be difficult to admit a weakness, divulge an intent to change, or seek support. A helping relationship between a supervisor and subordinate can look like favoritism. To avoid it, no one gets or seeks help, but this is truly harmful and foolish.

We have here another reason for supervisor training as part of any behavioral change program. Make sure supervisors recognize that learners may need sincere encouragement either from them or from others. When supervisors hold communication meetings, suggest that they talk about the helping relationships they will be hoping to see. Have them talk publicly about the help they intend to give, and the support they expect learners to receive when they ask for it (and even when they don't). Assuming everyone will be helpful is not a plan for success.

Sometimes it helps to write out a relationship agreement.

I am taking a leadership course, and I've elected to start with constructive listening. I will:

➤ Schedule enough time for one-on-one discussions so that my direct reports can comfortably express their thoughts without interruption.

➤ Pay full attention to what you are saying when you are speaking.

➤ Take time to understand what you have said and ask questions about any points that are unclear to me.

➤ Restate what you have said so that you can confirm that I heard and understood your thoughts.

➤ Not interrupt you while you are speaking, nor judge your ideas until I have fully considered them.

➤ Pause to consider what I am doing if you use appropriate hand signals to remind me of a violation of this plan.

relationship agreement continues on next page

relationship agreement continued from previous page

To help me, you will:

➢ Use hand signals to let me know immediately that I have violated one of my intentions, such as a finger across the throat to indicate that I have cut you off or a raised hand to indicate that you wish to inform me of how I am violating my intent.

➢ Give me honest feedback each time we meet about whether you feel I listened constructively, regardless of whether I agreed with you or made the decision you prefer.

Another idea is for learners to work with designated helpers who will schedule performance and feedback reviews. Learners should ask that some of the times scheduled for review will not be revealed in advance so that learners will need to be constantly vigilant.

One more idea. Have learners mentor other learners who are newer to the skill set than they are. Mentors will feel the need to set a good example, so it will help them maintain their own improved behaviors, and it will provide reviews of how to perform well. Just as one learns in-depth when having to teach, mentors will enjoy the benefits of vicarious practice and helping relationships when they work in support of other learners.

Blended learning

Many of the techniques suggested in this chapter and others are not typical of e-learning and aren't themselves e-solutions. They are about people helping people to achieve needed behavioral change. That said, with a little imagination, many of the techniques might be supported through technology and made not only easier to do, but also less expensive.

For example, electronic performance support techniques could easily be used in support of helping relationships. To assure that performance reviews are scheduled at times optimal for learning and actually happen as often as desired, automatic e-mail prompts or to-do list items can be generated by a software application and sent to the appropriate individuals, with copies sent to HR or supervisors. The software can transmit behavioral criteria to be used for evaluation and remind helpers how important it is to be supportive and honest at the same time. Interactive applications can assist helpers to prepare their reviews and even suggest ways feedback can be worded to be constructive.

There's a lot of current interest in blended learning, in part because so much e-learning fails to be meaningful, memorable, and motivational. It simply needs the help because of design inadequacies, not because e-learning couldn't do a much more effective job. On the other hand, there's nothing like effective, supportive, personal relationships to make life more meaningful and enjoyable. Unfortunately, when we need help undertaking the difficult task of behavioral change, people often don't know how to help best.

Simply adding more content presentations or providing live question-and-answer sessions, although these can be very helpful, does not develop the kind of blended learning that is really powerful. But extraordinarily better learning might come through blending the use of interactive technologies to support learners and their helpers in the overall process of behavioral change with the terrific e-learning instruction. Only a very little imagination is necessary to envision great opportunities here, but they clearly require us to *forget the usual boundaries of e-learning and think some very interesting thoughts.*

Summary

In this chapter, we looked at ways to enhance the likelihood that learned skills will be put to successful use. Although most instructional programs do not extend past delivery of courses and posttest measures, the transfer of learning to performance is a point at which the entire process is vulnerable.

Rather than focusing interventions on only the Instruction Phase, organizations need to design and develop aids to help learners transfer newly learned skills to performance. Techniques covered in this chapter are:

> Training supervisors to mentor

> Basing evaluation on observed performance

> Encouraging self-testing

> Teaching safety nets

> Providing refresher events and spaced practice

> Applying behavioral change techniques of reward, countering, controlling the environment, and helping relationships

Think Is classroom instruction typically so effective that we can improve e-learning b adding it to the "blend"?

Self-Assessment

Scenario 1: Hoboken Automotive Devices

Mark below what you think of Hoboken Automotive Devices' approach to e-learning now, after having read this book. Then compare your answers with both your initial answers recorded in Scenario 1 and with my answers, which appear in the next section. Try not to look ahead until you've actually written your own answers below.

Do you think Hoboken Automotive Devices is successful with their e-learning?

     O   Yes   O   No

For each of Margaret's requirements, check whether you think it was a good idea or a bad one. Note the reasons for your judgment.

Margaret's requirements	Good or bad requirement?	Basis for judgment
1. Courses are broken down into short modules, rarely requiring a learner to spend more than twenty minutes to complete each one.	O Good O Bad O Don't Know	Why?
2. Behavioral outcome objectives are listed for learners at the beginning of each module.	O Good O Bad O Don't Know	Why?

3. Lessons are highly interactive, requiring frequent user input. Game formats, such as Jeopardy or Wheel of Fortune, are used to keep learner interest high.

O Good

O Bad

O Don't Know

Why?

4. To gain positive learner reactions, challenge difficulty is kept low to minimize incorrect answers.

O Good

O Bad

O Don't Know

Why?

5. Task concepts and processes are presented clearly and demonstrated before learners are asked to perform them.

O Good

O Bad

O Don't Know

Why?

6. To make the procedures covered in the courses workable as corporate standards, content must be complete and suitable for new employees as well as for recurrent training.

O Good

O Bad

O Don't Know

Why?

Scenario 2: Water Mountain Beverage Company

Mark below what you think of Water Mountain Beverage Company's approach to e-learning now, after having read this book. Then compare your answers with both your initial answers recorded in Scenario 2 and with my answers, which appear in the next section. Try not to look ahead until you've actually written your own answers below.

Do you think Water Mountain Beverage Company is successful with their e-learning?

      ○   Yes   ○   No

For each of Ichiro's requirements, check whether you think it was a good idea or a bad one. Note the reasons for your judgment.

Ichiro's requirements	Good or bad requirement?	Basis for judgment
1. Clearly and accurately identify what learners need to know.	○ Good ○ Bad ○ Don't Know	Why?
2. Prepare posttests concurrent with (or even preceding) development of presentation content, so everyone will know what the target is.	○ Good ○ Bad ○ Don't Know	Why?

3. Use a modular structure with each module consisting of the following items in sequence: introduction, outline of basic points, elaboration of basic points, exercises with mentoring and available reference material, and posttest.

○ Good

○ Bad

○ Don't Know

Why?

4. Make text pages complete, accurate, and readable.

○ Good

○ Bad

○ Don't Know

Why?

5. Graduate exercises from easy to hard and precede each new type of problem or exercise with a demonstration.

○ Good

○ Bad

○ Don't Know

Why?

6. Provide immediate corrective feedback for each error and immediate confirmation of each correct response.	○ Good ○ Bad ○ Don't Know	Why?

Scenario 3: Top Tech Temps

Mark below what you think of TTT's approach to e-learning now, after having read this book. Then compare your answers with both your initial answers recorded in Scenario 3 and with my answers, which appear in the next section. Try not to look ahead until you've actually written your own answers below.

Do you think Top Tech Temps is successful with their e-learning?

○ Yes   ○ No

For each of Bill's requirements, check whether you think it was a good idea or a bad one. Note the reasons for your judgment.

Bill's requirements	Good or bad requirement?	Basis for judgment
1. Each project will have a marketing director who is responsible for creating corporate awareness and enthusiasm for the training program and what it will create.	○ Good ○ Bad ○ Don't Know	Why?

2. Each project will have a Mentoring and Performance Evaluation Program (MPEP) director.

- ○ Good
- ○ Bad
- ○ Don't Know

Why?

3. Each project will include a pre-instruction program to help learners prepare for learning and commit to excellent post-training support, even before they've begun training.

- ○ Good
- ○ Bad
- ○ Don't Know

Why?

4. Each project will include a training program that's as simple and interactive as possible. Every module of instruction will be meaningful, memorable, and motivational.

- ○ Good
- ○ Bad
- ○ Don't Know

Why?

Scenario 4: Bellmore University

Now that you've read the book, take a look at the top ten principles for designing an e-learning course on instructional design you listed on pages 17-19. Have you changed your mind, either thinking you would do something different now or drop them out of your top ten?

Take a moment to reread your initial list and comment below:

Your requirements   **Notes on modification or replacement**

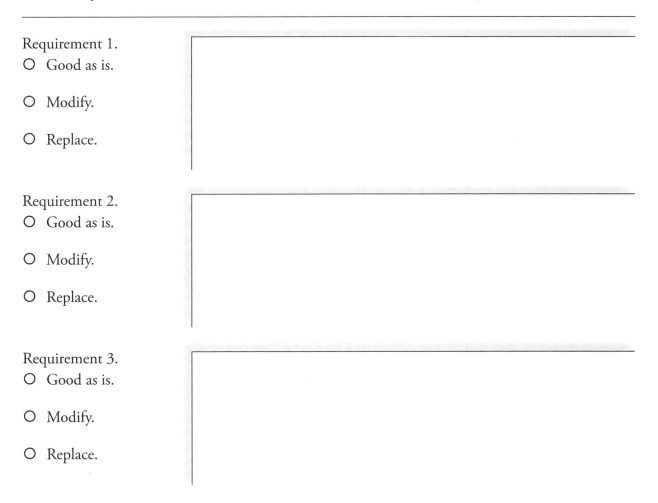

Requirement 1.
○ Good as is.

○ Modify.

○ Replace.

Requirement 2.
○ Good as is.

○ Modify.

○ Replace.

Requirement 3.
○ Good as is.

○ Modify.

○ Replace.

Requirement 4.
O Good as is.

O Modify.

O Replace.

Requirement 5.
O Good as is.

O Modify.

O Replace.

Requirement 6.
O Good as is.

O Modify.

O Replace.

Requirement 7.
O Good as is.

O Modify.

O Replace.

Requirement 8.
○ Good as is.

○ Modify.

○ Replace.

Requirement 9.
○ Good as is.

○ Modify.

○ Replace.

Requirement 10.
○ Good as is.

○ Modify.

○ Replace.

The recommendations of organizations cited in Scenarios 1, 2, and 3 are actual recommendations made by real companies, although the lists have been compiled from multiple organizations. Both the names of organizations and their training directors are aliases, and any similarity to actual organizations and persons of the same or similar names is entirely coincidental.

Scenario 1: Hoboken Automotive Devices

Was Hoboken Automotive Devices successful with their e-learning? It depends on how you define success. e-Learning has definitely reduced the costs of delivering training from what they were when they used only classroom training, at least the way they measured it. They didn't take on-the-job training costs or leadership failures into account. They didn't add in lost opportunities, costs of attrition, or expenses of responding to internal complaints of harassment.

So, from the executive office point of view, was the training successful?

       ⊙ **Yes**   ○ No

Learners were glad the lessons didn't last long, were easy to complete, and provided games where you could just guess and eventually get through them. From the learners' point of view, was the training successful?

       ⊙ **Yes**   ○ No

From my point of view, Margaret's requirements are based on popular instructional design concepts that are often misleading. For example, making courses short so the pain doesn't last as long addresses only the symptoms of design problems and does not fix the real problem at all. If designs are engaging and effective, the time to learn is time well spent. Sometimes longer sessions are much more valuable and even more enjoyable.

Hoboken Automotive Devices is gaining experience with e-learning and continually doing better. Do I think their e-learning is successful at this point?

○ Yes   ⊙ No

With respect to Margaret's list of requirements, here are my assessments, together with references in this book for further explanation and recommendation:

Margaret's requirements	Good or bad requirement?	Basis for judgment
1. Courses are broken down into short modules, rarely requiring a learner to spend more than twenty minutes to complete one.	○ Good ⊙ Bad ○ Don't Know	Why? Artificial requirement. Quick access is good; so if the learning modules were designed as just-in-time training, refresher training, or reference, making them short is very good. But a better requirement would have been to build strongly on context and create meaningful, memorable, and motivational learning experiences. Video games demonstrate that when this is done well, learning motivation can be maintained over a long period. Reference **Learning from games**, p. 181.

2. Behavioral outcome objectives are listed for learners at the beginning of each module.

○ Good

○ Bad

◉ Don't Know

Why? It depends on how the objectives are expressed. Most objective statements are boring. Learners quickly learn to skip them when they are.

Don't start out by boring your learners. Make objectives interesting, perhaps writing them into a storyline.

Reference **Using objectives to communicate with learners**, p. 111.

A better requirement would have been to build strongly on context and create meaningful, memorable, and motivational learning experiences. Video games demonstrate that when this is done well, learning motivation can be maintained over a long period.

Reference **Learning from games**, p. 181.

3. Lessons are highly interactive, requiring frequent user input; game formats, such as *Jeopordy* or *Wheel of Fortune* are used to keep learner interest high.

◉ Good

○ Bad

○ Don't Know

Why? Instructional interactivity isn't just requiring frequent input, it's causing learners to think and practice. Generalized game formats often make designs look more interactive than they are. Much better is to build on contexts that relate specifically to the content being taught.

Reference **Meaningful context**, p. 139, and **Approximating ideal activities**, p. 147.

4. To gain positive learner reactions, challenge difficulty is kept low to minimize incorrect answers.

○ Good

◉ Bad

○ Don't Know

Why? Challenges that provide some risk of error keep learners alert and involved. They allow learners the opportunity to learn from mistakes and often create far more interesting learning experiences that are also more memorable.

Reference **Risk**, p. 185.

5. Task concepts and processes are presented clearly and demonstrated before learners are asked to perform them.

○ Good

○ Bad

◉ Don't Know

Why? Demonstrations can be helpful and move learners ready for them along quickly. But demonstrations can also reduce the amount of analysis and thinking that can benefit learners. It's probably best to have demonstrations available, but encourage learners to see whether they can solve a problem without it first.

Reference **Demonstrations**, p. 168.

6. To use procedures covered in the courses as corporate standards, content is complete and suitable for new employees as well as for recurrent training.

○ Good

◉ Bad

○ Don't Know

Why? It's always tempting to strive for multiple uses of content, but they usually result in designs being compromised and less than optimal for anyone.

New learners need different levels and types of explanations and interactions than do those just needing a refresher.

Reference **Individualization**, p. 144.

Scenario 2: Water Mountain Beverage Company

Is Water Mountain Beverage Company successful with their e-learning? It depends on who you ask, but with the untapped enthusiasm and willing support the company provides, they are realizing far less of the opportunity than they could. The best answer is probably:

○ Yes ⦿ No

Ichiro doesn't include learners, subject-matter experts, and supervisors in project design unless it appears there are going to be problems. This means that assumptions are being made about important and difficult to assess things, such as what resonates with learners and what the skill deficits are. The design teams don't know what level of post-training support or interference to expect from supervisors. Training interventions aren't surrounded and supported by a change management campaign, so training is expected to accomplish much more than it typically can.

While it's great that the training director is popular and respected, and it's wonderful that the organization is ready to support change initiatives, the company is failing to realize their opportunities because of an aloof stance taken by the training department. It's important for training to get out and face the real world.

With respect to Ichiro's list of requirements, here are my assessments, together with references in this book for further explanation and recommendation:

Ichiro's requirements	Good or bad requirement?	Basis for judgment
1. Clearly and accurately identify what learners need to know.	⊙ Good ⊙ Bad ○ Don't Know	Why? Well, I cheated on this answer. This is a bad recommendation in that it focuses on what learners need to know and not what learners need to do. We need to focus first on what they need to do, but to prepare them to perform as desired, however, we do need also to identify what they need to know. Both are important, but the recommendation suggests a problematic focus. Reference **Success-based design**, p. 47, and **It's all about performance**, p. 197.
2. Prepare posttests concurrent with (or even preceding) development of presentation content, so everyone will know what the target is.	○ Good ⊙ Bad ○ Don't Know	Why? The target isn't good posttest scores; it's successful performance. Posttests tend to focus both designers and learners on an artificial learning task. Learners use a strategy that results in rapid forgetting subsequent to testing. The focus should be on transferring learning to real-world performance. Reference **Basing evaluation on observed performance**, p. 200, and **Teaching versus preaching**, p. 157.

3. Use a modular structure with each module consisting of the following items in sequence: an introduction, an outline of basic points, elaboration of basic points, exercises with mentoring and available reference material, and posttest.

○ Good

◉ Bad

○ Don't Know

Why? While this may sound like an excellent structure and would certainly make development systematic and easier, this content-centric approach is unlikely to create meaningful, memorable, and motivational experiences.

Reference **Working backward**, p. 143, and **Constructivism**, p. 42.

4. Make text pages complete, accurate, and readable.

◉ Good

○ Bad

○ Don't Know

Why? Although one shudders at the thought of a lot of text pages, they can be valuable resources. Minimalism cautions us, however, about putting too much into them. They should be brief and should not attempt to explain everything.

Reference **Minimalism**, p. 42.

5. Graduate exercises from easy to hard and precede each new type of problem or exercise with a demonstration.

○ Good

◉ Bad

○ Don't Know

Why? Again, while this approach systematizes design, it doesn't focus on the critical attributes of the learning experience. Often, more difficult exercises are more interesting to learners and motivate them to learn any basic skills they may not have. Better to start with interesting exercises, even if they are harder, and help learners develop basic skills in that context.

Reference **Working backward**, p. 143, and **Demonstrations**, p. 168.

6. Provide immediate corrective feedback for each error and immediate confirmation of each correct response.

○ Good

⊙ Bad

○ Don't Know

Why? Immediate feedback encourages guessing just to get the correct answer revealed. If the tactic works, learners don't bother to think and develop their abilities.

Reference **Delay judgment**, p. 190.

Scenario 3: Top Tech Temps

Is TTT successful with their e-learning? In a word:

⊙ **Yes**   ○ No

Remarkable transformations in the company's quality of service and productivity have resulted from the new, energetic training programs they've launched under Bill Hamm. The company as a whole has become performance focused. Actually, the company doesn't talk so much about having training programs. Instead, they view training as just one of the primary components of their "Top Performance Program" (TPP).

TPP campaigns begin with a flourish, commencing with preannouncements in their corporate blogs. T-shirts are given out in the cafeteria, where big banners celebrate the competitive achievements anticipated. Everyone in the company gets a t-shirt for each campaign, regardless of who is actually going to be learning and applying new skills, because TTT sees everyone as a participant in change. Everyone has at least a supportive role and is expected to cheer on and recognize the advancement of others.

Among all the positive benefits the company enjoys has been a significantly increased budget for learning-based programs, year after year. This, in turn, is producing even greater bottom-line benefits to TTT and all its stakeholders.

With respect to Bill's list of requirements, here are my assessments, together with references in this book for further explanation and recommendation:

Bill's requirements	Good or bad requirement?	Basis for judgment
1. Each project will have a marketing director who is responsible for creating corporate awareness and enthusiasm for the training program and what it will create.	⊙ Good ○ Bad ○ Don't Know	Why? Public awareness and support helps learners work on changing their behavior. It also encourages supervisors and peers to provide assistance and recognize progress. Having a marketing director will help make sure the campaign receives attention and isn't set aside while focus is put on designing instructional events. Reference **The campaign**, p. 91, and **Create a marketing plan**, p. 95.
2. Each project will have a Mentoring and Performance Evaluation Program (MPEP) director.	⊙ Good ○ Bad ○ Don't Know	Why? Preparing supervisors to mentor learners is one of those things that is often not done, either because no one thinks supervisors need help with this or thinks learners will need the help. Both are often program-defeating assumptions. Performance evaluation takes preparation and know-how. Putting someone in charge of this function may ensure that it gets the proper attention and execution. Reference **Training supervisors**, p. 199, **Helping relationships**, p. 205, and **Basing evaluation on observed performance**, p. 200.

3. Each project will include a pre-instruction program to help learners prepare for learning and commit to excellent post-training support, even before they've begun training.

⊙ Good

○ Bad

○ Don't Know

Why? Research on behavioral change indicates that people don't change their behaviors unless they are prepared and committed to the change. Similarly, people are likely to lapse into bad habits or easier behaviors if new skills aren't fully established.

Reference **Working the larger contexts**, p. 63, and **Designing Pre-Instructional Events**, p. 85.

4. Each project will include a training program that's as simple and interactive as possible. Every module of instruction will be meaningful, memorable, and motivational.

⊙ Good

○ Bad

○ Don't Know

Why? If learning programs aren't both meaningful and memorable, the learner's time is wasted. It won't have any impact on later performance. Similarly, if learners are not motivated to learn and apply their new skill, they won't. Again, time wasted and nothing accomplished.

Reference **The three Ms**, p. 50, **Meaningful events**, p. 137, **Memorable events**, p. 157, and **Motivational events**, p. 179.

Scenario 4: Bellmore University

Here's a list of ten recommendations you might consider. Compare these to your own list and then choose what you feel will be the best guidelines for your own projects. The "right" answers are those that work for you and produce learning experiences that succeed according to your definition of success.

Since I would want my students to be able to actually design effective learning experiences, not just recall what they've learned, my list is very much focused on what it will take to create skills and influence their behavior.

Michael's requirements	Reason for Requirement
1. Students will group into teams and be challenged to discuss and report 1) how they would assess their current instructional design abilities, 2) what they personally feel would be an outstanding success, and 3) what effort they are willing to put into the experience to make it successful. Teams should look at ways to use technology to facilitate communication among their members and to report to the whole of the class. Resources should be available to help learners assess their current abilities and think about what will be required to improve them.	I want to break down barriers that might retard informal learning, get learners to think about the changes in their skill sets that could occur with sufficient participation, and work learners toward making a commitment to success. Reference: **Maximizing informal learning**, p. 103, and **Facilitating change**, p. 90.

2. Objectives for the course will be written as if for a specific person whose experience and abilities will be described. Early task for learners will be to rewrite the objectives in the context of their own lives and dreams (of success), tailoring them to themselves, meeting the requirements of useful objectives, and making sure they have personal appeal.

Focus is critical for behavioral change and skill development, yet objectives are often boring and impersonal. This is a technique to overcome their typical shortcomings while helping learners better prepare themselves for involvement, commitment, and change.

Reference **Writing objectives that are useful**, p. 113.

3. Initial learning experiences will get right to the point: Learners will be asked to analyze a variety of learning experiences to 1) describe what is good about them, 2) describe what is bad, and 3) state how they would rectify all identified problems to make each experience a successful one.

I want to keep things interesting and build on initial motivation and energy. People often think instructional design is intuitive and something they can do well without much guidance. Let's see how similar or divergent the group's thinking is, and set a baseline for growth.

Reference **Challenge**, p. 130, and **Motivational challenge**, p. 185.

4. A teaching assistant's role will be defined as a learning campaign manager. Duties will include blogging interviews with class participants, highlighting the progress of projects, soliciting and reporting project appraisals by other faculty members, and reporting comments by family members and/or employers on what they know of the class's work.

We want to make the experience as relevant as possible. It needs to be "real world," not just academic. And we also want the reinforcement and encouragement of others. In addition, the more public exposure will help keep learners motivated to do their best and follow through.

Reference **Facilitating change**, p. 90.

5. Learners will be given a series of interesting on-line design challenges. They will have selectable as well as open-end choices, which are forwardd to the instructor. Feed back will come through simulated learner responses and behaviors selected by the instructor, but no judgment or hints will be given. Learners will have links to relevant resource materials. If they are stuck and can't get positive results, the application will suggest they contact other students (and provide aids to do so).

Intrinsic feedback is powerful. Because I want my students to focus on getting learners to do the things that will really help them develop and apply new skills, I don't want to give feedback that implies the goal is really getting my (or the instructor's) approval.

Instructors will certainly talk with them, but encouraging informal learning through discussion with other students can provide another level of help.

Reference **Meaningful feedback**, p. 151.

6. As students create design solutions, a "Leader Board" will post the results of the five highest scores so far (by student name).

Because the intrinsic feedback might just reveal how well designs are working, but not necessarily the highest level of achievement possible, students are encouraged to keep exploring. As they see the scores of others moving higher and higher, they should be motivated to keep improving their own work.

Reference **Motivational feedback**, p. 190.

7. Major challenges will be accompanied by short, small task exercises, such as discriminating between examples of intrinsic and extrinsic feedback. These repetitive exercises will run throughout the term and be spaced further and further apart.

Spaced practice is more resistant to extinction. I want to be sure my students are strong in the fundamentals.

Reference **Spaced learning events**, p. 76 and Provide **spaced practice**, p. 173.

8. Easer, novel, and/or humorous exercises, at both the major and minor task levels, will be interspersed with those of steadily increasing difficulty.	It's important to build confidence and enjoy the power newly acquired skills impart. We'll take time to revel in capabilities and practice their application before heading upward into the next level of challenge. Reference **Selecting the right content for each learner**, p. 186.
9. Students having completed the course will be eligible for extra credit by mentoring learners in the course. A prerequisite will be completing a short interactive primer on mentoring.	We learn a lot from mentoring and mentored learners have better success in applying their new skills. This is a technique to kick start both. Reference **Mentoring**, p. 199.
10. The final project will be to design a course for the e-Learning for Kids Foundation.	e-Learning for Kids is a global non-profit foundation taking the best of learning technology to children from five to twelve years of age wherever they can be reached. Its mission is to acquire the best of the best in learning technology, donated by industry professionals, and make it available free. This is an inspiring movement, and while beginning designers may not be up to the task of designing the highest quality e-learning, taking a stab at it is a motivational challenge that can supercharge talent development. Reference **Build outcome anticipation**, p. 182, and **e-learningforkids.org**.

A Final Word

The e-learning industry has grown and changed dramatically. Throughout what has now become decades of work for me, the men and women who also work so passionately in this field have been not only patient but also supportive of my rants and raves. I am so very grateful for the good humor, support and encouragement I've received.

Undaunted, I'm continually pushing for reform. This book presents perhaps my hardest push, because in researching and writing it, the task brought together a perspective and some solutions I've been searching for. It's based on the realization that even perfectly designed e-learning, as we've defined it in the past, isn't sufficient to achieve the behavioral changes it's being used for.

I'll admit I'm a bit out on a limb here. And yet I see experience, theory, and research aligning and pointing us in a new and very promising direction. The reality of a learner's life (recognized by the champions of informal learning), the difficulty of change (that psychotherapists recognize), and the amazing powers of intrigue and motivation (that video game designers harness) can and should be synthesized as the foundation for the new era of e-learning design.

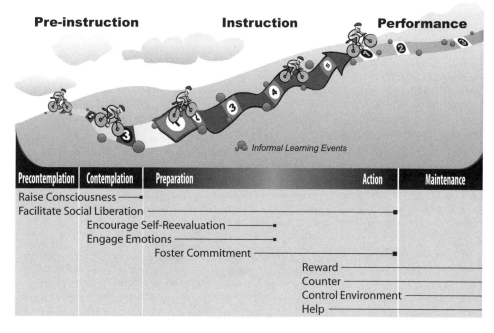

My hope is that this book serves as a useful step to help us all move more effectively in new design directions.

MWA

Index

A

Achievement Principle, 190

Action stage, 68, 72

Activities: as design components, 132–133; authenticity and fidelity, 149; examples of poor and better, 133; as interactivity design component, 195; matching objectives to, 146–147; meaningful, 145–151; memorable, 159, 170–173; motivational, 189–190

Adaptive feedback and review paradigm for computer-based drills (Siegel and Misselt), 193

ADDIE Model, 29

Advanced Web-Based Training Strategies: (Driscoll and Carliner), 39

Alessi, S. M., 30, 31, 40, 43, 154

Aligning Stages of Change, 71–73

Allen, M. W., 63, 79, 128, 129

Amplification of Input Principle, 190

Animation and learning: Value for money? (Lowe), 164

Assessment: pre-instructional phase self-assessment, 107–108; scenario self-assessment, 209–217; scenario success, 219–232

The ASTD Handbook of Instructional Technology (Piskurich), 154

Atkinson, R., 164

Attention density, 203

Authenticity, 149

B

Backgrounding: described, 109–111; primary questions to answer when, 111–113

Bahrick, H. P., 76

Bam! EEEEEK! POW! What video games can teach us about e-learning feedback (Dirksen presentation), 187

Bane, D., 199

Behavior change facilitation: encouraging self-reevaluation for, 90–91, 98–100, 107–108; engaging emotions for, 91, 100–101; establishing campaign logo for, 106; facilitating social liberation for, 90, 96–98, 106; fostering commitment for, 91, 101–102; raising learner consciousness for, 90, 91–96; steps in, 90–91

Behavioral change: applying techniques for, 202–206; design challenge for, 65–66; e-learning for achieving, 106-108; improving instructional interventions for, 59, 90–91; instructional design and psychology of, 23; meaningful context targeting specific, 139; physiological evidence of resistance to, 89–90; pre-instructional events to facilitate, 85; psychology of, 66–74; research on difficulty of, 57, 89–90; resource on, 66

Behavioral change psychology: overview of, 66–67; parallels to learning for performance improvement, 69–71; Stages of Change model, 67–69, 71–74

Behavioral patterns: accumulating influences shaping, 65; design challenge for changing, 65–66; designing e-learning in context of, 81; "jaywalking" segment on oblivious, 101; looking for determinants of, 112–113; performance problems associated with, 111–112

Behaviorism, cognitivism, constructivism: (Ertmer and Newby), 49

Behaviorism design approach: described, 39–41; success-based design using, 48

Bellezza, F. S., 166

Bellmore University scenario: background information on, 17; e-learning requirements for, 18–19; self-assessment of, 215–217; success assessment of, 229–232

Beyond the Comfort Zone: (Atkinson, McBeath, Jonas-Dwyer, and Phillips), 164

Bichelmeyer, B., 30

The Big (32") Picture of informal learning (Cross), 104

Bitzer, D., 172

Blended learning, 79–80, 206–207

Boehle, S., 36

Boyle, T., 40, 43

Brain teaser, 169

Brainstorming sessions, 56

Branch, R. M., 30, 31

Budget (pre-instruction phase), 87–88, 104–105

Building Codes Illustrated: (Ching and Winkel), 122

Building helpful relationships, 205–206

C

Carey, S., 29

Carliner, S., 29, 38, 39

Carroll, J. M., 42, 43

Challenge: as design component, 130, 132; examples of poor and better, 131; as interactivity design component, 195; meaningful, 143–145; memorable, 159, 166–170; motivational, 185–189

Change campaign: creating the message for, 92–93; marketing the message, 94–96; sample marketing plan for, 96

Changing for Good: (Prochaska, Norcross, and DiClemente), 66

Child Development, 183

Ching, F.D.K., 122

CIO Magazine, 89

Clark, D., 113, 114, 115

Cognitive approaches to instructional design (Wilson, Jonassen, and Cole), 154

Cognitivism (design approach): described, 41–42; meaningful learning events using, 153; memorable learning events using, 176; motivational learning events using, 194; success-based design using, 48

Cole, P., 154

Commitment to change, 91, 101–102

Communication: learnscaping through, 103–104; using objectives as, 117–118

Competitive teams, 101

The Conditions of Learning (Gagné), 115

The Conditions of Learning: Training Applications (Gagné and Medsker), 43

Consolidation process, 173

Constructivism (design approach): described, 42–43; meaningful learning events using, 153; memorable learning events using, 176; motivational learning events using, 194–195; success-based design using, 48

Contemplation stage, 67, 72, 108

Content, 36

Context: common oversights regarding, 142–143; convoluted, 142; described, 130; examples of poor and better, 131; as interactivity design component, 195; meaningful, 139–143; memorable, 159, 160–166; motivational, 181–185

Controlling the environment, 204–205

Convoluted contexts, 142

Corrective Feedback Paradigm (CFP), 193–194

Countering, 203–204

CPR activity, 147, 149

Creating Successful e-Learning—A Rapid System for Getting It Right First Time, Every Time, 55, 110

Cross, J., 62, 78, 103, 104

D

Damarin, S., 30, 31

Demonstrations, 168–169

The Design, Development, and Evaluation of Instructional Software (Hannafin and Peck), 30

Design for Multimedia Learning (Boyle), 43

Designing performance aids. *See* Performance aids

Dick and Carey Model, 29

Dick, W., 29

DiClemente, C., 66, 69

Dirksen, J., 187

Discovery Principle, 185–186

Discussion facilitation, 104

Doppler effect, 163

Dornbush, R. L., 183

Dragging activities, 150

Dramatic feedback, 175–176

Driscoll, M., 38, 39

Index

Index

About Allen Interactions Inc.

Allen Interactions was formed by learning technology pioneers who have continuously created precedent-setting learning solutions since the late 1960s. Their award-winning custom design and development services have been commissioned by Apple Inc., American Express, Bank of America, Boston Scientific, Delta Air Lines, Disney, Ecolab, IBM, Medtronic, Merck, Microsoft, Motorola, Nextel, UPS, and hundreds of other leading corporations.

Working with IBM and then with Control Data Corporation, Michael Allen led the development of the first two widely used LMS systems. His pioneering work on visual authoring systems led to the ground-breaking introduction of Authorware, elevated the level of interactivity that educators could develop, and launched Macromedia, together with a new industry of interactive multimedia tools.

Now, his studios at Allen Interactions carry on the search for more meaningful, memorable, and motivational instructional paradigms, faster and lower-cost methods of designing and building technology-enhanced learning solutions, and ways to share their discoveries with those interested in more effective learning.

About the Author

g his work in technology-enhanced learning at Cornell College in the late ₒₒ0s, he has been developing instructional paradigms, systems, and innovative tools ever since. Michael W. Allen holds M.A. and Ph.D. degrees in educational psychology from The Ohio State University. He is an adjunct associate professor at the University of Minnesota Medical School in the Department of Family Medicine and Community Health.

Active in e-learning organizations, publishing, and speaking, he has consulted internationally with governments and major corporations on the use of technology for learning. Dr. Allen created the first commercial LMS products used internationally, the precedent-setting visual authoring tool, Authorware, and countless instructional applications. His first book, *Michael Allen's Guide to e-Learning: Building interactive, fun, and effective learning programs for any company,* has been praised by beginners and experts alike. Dr. Allen's advice is based on unrivaled experience and insights.